The Flamboya Tree

Clara Olink Kelly now lives in Bellingham, Washington with her husband. She spends much of her time with her children and grandchildren. *The Flamboya Tree* is her first book.

'Incredibly moving . . . The courage of the whole family, particularly of Clara's mother, shines through' Cathy Kelly, *Daily Mail*

'Fascinating' *People Magazine*

'A wrenching memoir . . . These stories clearly demonstrate that terrible atrocities are committed – justified even – in the name of war' *Seattle Times*

'A moving, immediate account of a relatively unknown wartime drama . . . Unforgettable' *Booklist*

'Remarkable . . . *The Flamboya Tree* charts a family journey that is awesome and heartbreaking, but which remains a story of hope' *The Herald Sun*

'An affecting account of wartime deprivation . . . Well written' *Publishers Weekly*

'*The Flamboya Tree* is a touching story of how a mother's love saved a family of three defenseless children trapped in a brutal Japanese death camp. As Clara Kelly honours her mother's memory we are reminded that not all the heroes of World War II faced the bullets of the battle-field' James Bradley

'Nothing illustrates wartime suffering and sacrifices more poignantly than a child's voice. Clara Kelly has done a wonderful job capturing the depravity of the Java prison camps and the courage of interned mothers trying to keep their young children alive and humane. *The Flamboya Tree* is a fascinating story that will leave the reader informed about a missing piece of the World War II experience, and in awe of one family's survival' Elizabeth Norman

'*The Flamboya Tree* is like a bright jewel found in the dust of fading history. I was bowled over by this book' Caroyln See

'Simply told, deeply felt, Kelly's *The Flamboya Tree* shows us that adversity can transform our lives into courageous, life-affirming works of art' Gwyn Hyman Rubio

'Sometimes the history of war hides its best stories, its fine, quiet stories . . . *The Flamboya Tree* is such a story, with some kinship to Nicholas Gage's *Eleni*, and, in the same extraordinary way, about the triumph of love and compassion and decency' Alan Furst

'Surefooted and bighearted, Kelly's narrative offers testimony to the sustaining power of dignity and courage in the face of impossible circumstances' Beth Kephart, author of *A Slant of Sun*

The Flamboya Tree

A Family's War-time Courage

Clara Olink Kelly

arrow books

Published in the United Kingdom by Arrow Books in 2003

7 9 10 8 6

First published by Random House Trade Publishing,
a division of Random House Inc.

Arrow Books
Random House, 20 Vauxhall Bridge Road,
London SW1V 2SA

Random House Australia (Pty) Limited
20 Alfred Street, Milsons Point, Sydney,
New South Wales 2061, Australia

Random House New Zealand Limited
18 Poland Road, Glenfield,
Auckland 10, New Zealand

Random House (Pty) Limited
Endulini, 5a Jubilee Road, Parktown 2193, South Africa

The Random House Group Limited Reg. No. 954009

www.randomhouse.co.uk

A CIP catalogue record for this book is available from the British Library

Papers used by The Random House Group are natural, recyclable
products made from wood grown in sustainable forests; the manufacturing processes
conform to the environmental regulations of the country of origin

Typeset by Palimpsest Book Production Limited,
Polmont, Stirlingshire
Printed and bound in Great Britain by
Bookmarque, Croydon, Surrey

ISBN 0 09 944553 0

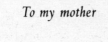
To my mother

It is not easy to remember
    that in the fading light of day —
        the shadows always point toward
the dawn.

Let
   me
      remember
beyond forgetting —
      let
       me
        remember —

          —

          —

Winston O. Abbott

Contents

Introduction

It is a well-known fact that war, any war, is senseless and degrading. When innocent people are brought into that war because they happen to be in the wrong place at the wrong time, it becomes incomprehensible. Java, 1942, was such a place and time, and we were those innocent people.

As part of its strategy to become the largest and most important empire in the world, Japan had successfully seized Manchuria from China and now sought control of North China and Mongolia to protect Manchuria. However, China was not about to relinquish any more territory to Japan and was willing to fight till the bitter end. Therefore, Japan had to ensure that no reinforcements or supplies could enter China from the outside world. In order to do this, Japan had to control all the islands of the South Pacific and the Dutch East Indies, which included Java. These were islands rich in natural resources and, most important, oil. Japan was in need of these precious commodities. Since the United States was cutting off all supplies of oil, Japan realized that control of the islands was absolutely imperative to the success of the Imperial Empire. Invasion was inevitable.

Unfortunately, the Japanese fleets, both on the sea and in the air, were too large and too well trained for the Dutch to be able to defend their islands for very long. Once the Japanese had invaded, escape was impossible.

While the war in the South Pacific and the Dutch East Indies was escalating, so, too, was Hitler's war in Europe. The United States had hoped that diplomatic measures with Japan could avert further problems, but talks broke down when Japan attacked Pearl Harbor. America entered the war, and World War II became a reality.

The beautiful life on these islands filled with flowers, fruits, lush vegetation, and soft-spoken, gentle people was suddenly transformed into a life of indescribable horror over which none of us had control.

Once the Japanese had invaded the islands, they had to make sure the citizens, who included Dutch, British, New Zealanders, and Australians, would not hinder them in any way. They chose to capture and imprison close to eighty-five thousand citizens living on the island of Java by incarcerating them in concentration camps. Whole sections of towns and villages were surrounded by fences of barbwire, guarded and patrolled day and night by Japanese soldiers.

The men and teenage boys were taken away to labor camps. Many, including my father, were forced to work on the Burma railroad and deep inside the sweltering jungles. This was the railroad that lead to the bridge on the river Kwai, where so many prisoners died due to the extreme cruelties and hardships they suffered at the hands of the Japanese. My father, for one, would never talk about the violence except to explain that he was so severely beaten around the head that he lost part of his hearing.

The women and children were crowded into the concentration camps. At first there were sixty to seventy people in a single home. Those numbers would double by the end of the war. Tens of thousands of women and children were forced to endure a life no one could have imagined: stress and sickness from overcrowding, filth, and extreme malnutrition. This was the life my family had to bear for almost four years.

We had the misfortune of being placed in Kamp Tjideng, notoriously the worst camp among all the women's camps. The number of prisoners here totaled ten thousand for the first year or so and was gradually increased as time went on. Not only were more and more prisoners brought into camp, but space and houses were also taken away as the barbwire fences tightened into an ever-decreasing circle, adding to the already overstressed situation. Cruel and inhumane treatment in this camp, instigated by the sadistic Lieutenant Sonei, the camp commandant, was a daily routine. Worse than that, however, was the knowledge that you were slowly and methodically being starved to death at the will of the Japanese, because in their eyes your life was worthless. I can imagine no worse nightmare for a young mother, my mother, than the realization that her three small children may die because food is being withheld through no fault of their own. What terrible anguish she must have felt, knowing that her children's lives depended entirely on her, and yet she, as the mother, was unable to help them because she herself was at the mercy of her captors.

It is these daily struggles to survive that I try to describe in this book. This is a period in history that some people know nothing about, and when I'm gone, the stories, too, would otherwise be lost forever. To this day, Japan denies that these atrocities ever happened. Japanese children are not taught about the war in school, and there are no history books recounting even minor details of the Japanese involvement with the concentration camps on the islands. Though the prisoners who survived these terrible ordeals continue to ask for an apology from the Japanese government, we know that we will never get one.

'This was *your* war,' we are told. 'It has nothing to do with us.'

We survived our internment and were able to lead relatively normal, happy lives after the war, thanks to our mother's courage and determination to bring us safely through those difficult years.

Even though I don't consciously think about the camp all the time, it lives in the back of my mind. I'm often reminded of things that happened and have told my children and now my grandchildren as well. I want them to know about that period of my life. I hope it might teach them that with a strong will, they, too, can get through some of the tougher times that are bound to enter into their lives. Over and over again, they've asked me to write the stories down.

It was difficult at first. The whole experience was like a horrendous nightmare that I thought I would rather forget. But as I started to sift through the stories, I realized that there were also moments of great tenderness, love, and joy interspersed among the times of terror and hopelessness. I admit I shed quite a few tears when some of the memories came flooding back. Tears of sorrow for my mother, mostly. Sorrow that she had to endure this suffering on her own.

I like to think that she looks down now from wherever she is and smiles as I pay tribute to her indomitable spirit and her unfaltering humanity.

The Flamboya Tree

1

Holland, 1946

'Why didn't you try to escape?'

That was all she said. Not 'Thank God you made it. Now you are safe.'

'Why didn't you try to escape?'

Why was she saying that? She was supposed to be so happy to see us. I saw again in my mind's eye the barbwire fences and the soldiers with their glistening bayonets, and felt once more that excruciating fear in the pit of my stomach. Try to escape? Lots of people had *tried* to escape.

I pushed the brutal memory from my mind. How long had we lived for this very moment? Through all those years, the words 'when we get back to Holland' had sustained us. There had been no doubt in our minds that one day we *would* return to Holland to meet aunts and uncles, as well as cousins our own age. We had talked about celebrations with real cakes, and cookies, and lemonade. It was going to be such a happy time. I had imagined my grandmother telling us how lovely it was to see us at last. How big we'd grown, how pretty and handsome we looked. We had never met her, though we had heard so many wonderful tales about her. And now here we were in Holland, standing on her doorstep, and all we could do was stare at one another as though we were all waiting for something very special to happen.

Why hadn't we tried to escape?

It felt like a rebuke. We must not have tried hard enough. I looked over at my mother, wanting to protect her from the harsh words. My poor, sweet mother was obviously in a lot of pain, standing there on her infected, swollen legs. Sometimes she could hardly walk on them, let alone run. And wasn't that what you did when you tried to escape – run? Run as fast as you could? Glancing back at my grandmother, I began to feel very uncomfortable. She was standing there studying each of us in turn. Our pasty yellow skin and sunken eyes. Our bones sticking out through our worn, donated clothes. And worst of all, our filthy, lice-infested heads. She saw it all, and her eyes welled with tears.

My mother, my two brothers, Willem and Gijs, and I had only that day returned to Holland, my mother's homeland, after spending more than three and a half years in a Japanese concentration camp in the Dutch East Indies. We were not a pretty sight, and we had caught my grandmother completely off guard.

The ambulance drivers who had brought us here from the boat finally broke the awkward silence. They were still carrying the stretcher on which my oldest brother, Willem, lay covered with blankets. He was extremely ill with double pneumonia, and they were anxious to get him out of the damp, chilly air. My grandmother pulled herself upright and immediately motioned us all to come into the house. Gijs and I held tightly to each other's hands and followed closely behind our mother as she hobbled painfully up the stone steps. Her beriberi was so bad by this time that she could probably not have survived more than a few months longer in the concentration camp.

'Is this another camp?' Gijs asked once we were inside and he had looked all around. 'Where are the other people?'

Having been born just weeks before we were interned,

he had grown up in the camps and had known only those overcrowded, filthy conditions as the way of life. This large, empty house was alien to him, as well as to me. We expected a horde of people to appear from every doorway.

As we milled around in the spacious hall, my grandmother asked the ambulance men to follow her upstairs with the stretcher so Willem could be put to bed. She was taken aback when Willem protested vehemently. Sick as he was, he was desperately trying to get off the stretcher to stay with us. My mother rushed to his side to reassure him and asked that he be allowed to lie in the same room where we would all be. Our many years of living in fear now made us want to stick close together.

While all this was going on, Gijs and I glanced nervously up the curving staircase to watch for anyone else up there. We could not believe that our grandmother lived all alone in such a big house. Our grandfather had died when our mother was just a young girl.

Many doorways opened off the hallway. Oriental carpets covered the hardwood floors, and ornate polished furniture filled the rooms. Everything shone and sparkled with a cleanliness unknown to us, as we had concentrated on simply staying alive. In the living room, little tables covered in pretty embroidered cloths stood ready to serve dainty sweets and teas from silver teapots. Our eyes focused immediately on the sugar lumps in the silver bowl.

'You may take one,' our grandmother said with a smile. But I didn't dare. It was Gijs who quickly reached over and ravenously grabbed three, one for each of us.

'My God, what happened to you?' was all our grandmother could whisper as she shook her head in disbelief.

We watched her silently from a safe distance. Our mother gave a big sigh and stared out of the window. 'Let me relax for a while,' she said, 'then I will try to explain.'

It was obviously very difficult for my grandmother to accept our appalling condition, and she must have wanted to do something straightaway to rectify the injustices and hurts inflicted on her family by a cruel war. We must have seemed so unapproachable and scared, when all she wanted to do was make us feel welcome and safe. She was not able to simply stand back and let us be. She had no idea what we had been through, and so she again made the suggestion that we children go upstairs to see the surprises she had prepared for us. Surely gifts could ease some of the pain in our hearts, as well as hers.

Her kind invitation was again met with strong opposition. There was absolutely no way we were going anywhere with someone who, at this point, was a complete stranger. We didn't know what was up there. We were too wary of danger lurking around every corner.

'Why don't you bring the surprises downstairs so we can all see them,' my mother suggested.

After thinking about it, our grandmother left the room. This eased the tension, and we nervously looked around. It was all very overwhelming. There were big oil paintings of Dutch country scenes hanging on the walls, while an ornately carved wooden floor lamp of a bird-of-paradise stood in the corner beside a piano. The long silk tassels hanging from the lamp shade rippled gently in the slightest breeze. A small gilt clock on the marble mantel chimed every half hour, while the pendulum with four shiny balls rotated first one way, then the other. I was mesmerized by it.

From the living room where we sat, huge sliding doors disappeared into the walls that opened to a sunroom. Wicker furniture with plump, flowered cushions stood on the tiled floor. Another tea table stood ready with a china tea set. Beyond the sunroom lay the garden. I was surprised to see another little house nestled among the trees.

'A little garden house,' my grandmother called it, 'for quiet moments.'

It would become one of my favorite places to play, among the comfortable chaise longues where you could lie and page endlessly through wonderful picture books. When my mother's old dolls were unpacked from a wooden trunk in the attic and brought to the little house for me to play with, I felt that my happiness was truly complete, that I never wanted to leave this heavenly place. But that feeling was many, many months away yet.

Our grandmother returned from upstairs with several packages in her arms. Sticking close to our mother's side, we watched as she laid them in front of us on the table. For Willem, she had bought some boys' adventure books that couldn't have delighted him more, as he loved to read. For Gijs she brought a wooden toy. I received a cloth doll, complete with every imaginable outfit, from underwear and nightdresses to coats and hats and shoes. She had made everything except the hard china head, for which she had paid a lot of money in a toy shop. The doll and her clothes were beautiful, but I could never learn to love her. Her face was so serious, I always thought she was angry. It must have been very disappointing for my grandmother, who tried so hard to encourage me to play with her instead of hiding her under the bed.

––––––––

For a while we sat in her living room and stared at one another without saying a word. Our tattered old suitcase stood on the floor between my legs, and my grandmother's eyes focused on the string around it.

'What do you have in there, Claartje?'

'Our painting.'

'May I see it?'

I fingered the string but did not untie it.

'What else do you have in there?' my grandmother asked as she reached for the suitcase.

'Nothing. Just the painting.' I stood up as she removed the string and opened the lid. Glancing furtively around the room, I edged my way over to stand beside her. She hesitated before sticking her hand into the case to take out the painting. Holding it at arm's length, she studied it with her lips tightly pursed. Without a word, she was about to put it down on the floor when I grabbed the painting and hastily returned to the couch beside my mother.

'Why do you have that painting? Where are your other things?' My grandmother sounded annoyed that we had bothered to bring back such a worthless article.

'That painting is very dear to me,' my mother answered slowly. 'It is the only article that was *not* useful when I packed to go into the camp. It restored my soul when times got ugly.' She turned and gazed wistfully at the painting in my lap and said, 'Don't you think the flamboya tree is very beautiful?'

2

Bandung, Java, 1942

It was early morning, still dark and cool in the bedroom of the bungalow where we lived in Bandung, on the island of Java, in the Dutch East Indies. As sunlight filtered in around the closed curtains, I was eager to get up.

I did not like sleeping in this bedroom, which I shared with my older brother, Willem. There was a trapdoor in the ceiling, and our *baboe,* the Indonesian nursemaid, had told us that if we did not behave and go to sleep right away, it would open and a big gorilla would jump out to drag us back into the ceiling with him. I was only four years old and so petrified that this might happen, I insisted our beds be pushed close together, side by side. I would lie on my back, sucking my thumb, and stare at that trapdoor until I finally fell asleep. My mother could not understand why I was so afraid, and I could not tell her about the gorilla, because Baboe had assured me the gorilla would be very angry indeed if I told anyone where it lived.

This morning I lay in bed and listened to the *scritch-scritch* of the gardener's rake as he straightened the gravel around the house. He did this twice a day, morning and evening, so the paths always looked smooth and tidy. It was a comforting sound to me in those early hours of the morning, although I had no way of knowing that even this comforting sound was about to change. That the impending war would give the crunching of gravel a completely different meaning.

I crawled out of bed and ran to the window. Pushing a curtain aside, I stared at the house across the road, waiting for what I knew would start at any moment: the lady singing in her shower to the accompaniment of the flowing water. I pushed the window open a little more to get a better smell. It was not only her singing that appealed to me, it was the glorious fragrance of her soap. It floated out her window on the notes of her songs. My mother used to laugh and say, 'She must be practicing for the opera.' I don't think she liked this lady's voice much, but to me she was special because of her wonderfully fragrant soap. And best of all, once her singing started, I felt safe and assured. A new day had begun, and people were about. I knew that the gorilla never came out during the day.

Our bungalow was always cool and quiet. The servants silently came and went on bare feet across the stone floors. Running all the way around the house was a big veranda where tea was served in the afternoons, overlooking the lawns that rolled down to the wide, muddy river. There was always something happening on the river. On most days it was only the sampans, floating lazily by on the way to market, loaded with fish or fruit and vegetables, but on this day the river came alive with hundreds of boats of all sizes festooned with bright ribbons and flags and paper lanterns. Indonesians loved festivals and were always celebrating some event. This day the birth of a baby into a prominent tribal family was the cause for all the excitement and everyone was invited. People dressed up in wondrous costumes with enormous masks pulled over their heads, danced and somersaulted with boundless energy. Stilt-walkers strode audaciously from one teetering boat onto the next, while dressed-up monkeys performed clever tricks balanced on long poles.

Our parents watched from the veranda as the afternoon waned, and though they didn't seem to be enjoying the loud music and high-pitched singing that accompanied every wave of boats, Willem and I were entranced. We were also very aware of the delicious aromas emanating from the sampans.

We knew that each one carried its own offerings of delectable foods: fried pork or morsels of roasted chicken dipped in spicy peanut sauce. Fried bananas, rice cakes, roast duck, or dried fish. It was more than we could resist. We begged our parents to send the *djongos,* our Indonesian houseboys, down to the river to buy some of that delicious food for us, but they told us that would not be wise, as we did not know how it was prepared. It wasn't clean, they said.

Finally, with dark came the fireworks. Beautiful works of art, they boomed and cracked and screeched overhead. They lit up the skies in radiant colors only to rain down into the water and disappear forever. We shuddered with delight and fear. The explosions were terribly loud to us, and we blocked our ears with our fists but could still feel the vibrations in our chests.

The celebrations on the river were becoming more riotous. A brightly painted canoe paddled to a spot on the river right in front of our house, and it was obvious the party intended to put on a show especially for our benefit. Three men, their bodies decorated in the bright stripes representing forest warriors, were sitting in the canoe. Slowly, they rose as though stalking prey. We watched them, mesmerized. Turning this way and that, they battled the unseen enemy as the canoe rocked and tilted dangerously.

Suddenly, the canoe turned completely upside down and threw the brave warriors into the water. Willem jumped up from his seat and screamed in panic as the canoe continued to drift down the river. Just when we thought all was lost, three sets of hands rose out of the water and righted the canoe. The glistening-wet warriors slid silently back over the sides and paddled on, to loud applause from the opposite riverbank. My six-year-old brother, Willem, was inconsolable. Petrified that the warriors had drowned, he had not, through his tears, seen them climb back into the canoe.

The teeming life on the river fascinated us children, but not so our parents. They often scanned that river up and down, speaking in worried voices about 'them,' the Japanese, possibly coming up the river in boats. Many times they cursed the river for being so close to the house.

'They could sneak up the back way before we would even know they were there,' I heard them whisper.

I began to look at that river with a bit more fear in my heart. What could possibly come crawling out of it to our cozy house?

It was not only what was happening on the river that seemed to be of concern, but also what was happening in the sky. More and more frequently now, planes bearing the Japanese insignia of the Rising Sun droned overhead. My parents would stare up at the planes without saying a word. Just by their silence, Willem and I knew that the planes were not a welcome sight.

———

For a time my father's work kept him too busy to dwell on these worries. He was the managing director of the Indonesian branch of the Holland-Colombo Trading Society, which had been started by my grandfather. From this office, spices, teas, coffee, cocoa beans, and large sheets of rubber tapped from the local rubber plantations were shipped to Europe and England. The company was originally started in Ceylon, now called Sri Lanka, where my father worked for several years and where both Willem and I were born. He was then transferred to Java when I was still a baby.

It was a wonderful life on the island for the many European and British settlers, most of whom had come over to own or run the vast tobacco, rubber, tea, or sugar plantations. Still others were in charge of the oil refineries. Large modern cities sprang up to house these well-to-do citizens, and a Dutch colonial government took over.

The hot, tropical climate was difficult to get used to. The high humidity and extreme heat made it hard for European transplants to work normal hours. A workday usually started around six A.M. and finished by noon, when everyone went home for a nap. Even the schools stuck to those hours.

The scenery was lush and exotic. Palm trees, hibiscus, and bougainvillea vines flourished, and there was always an abundance of fresh fruits and vegetables.

Servants were cheap, and they proved faithful and loyal workers for those *blandas,* whites or Europeans, who treated them well. Life with the *blandas* was a lot easier than working on the plantations. For the Indonesian women, who mostly worked in the paddy fields – large terraces of water in which they had to stand all day long, bent over to plant the tender rice shoots – work in a *blanda* home was definitely a welcome and prized position.

But in a country where there was so much poverty,

these lifestyles did not come without a price. Resentment was growing among the native people against the outsiders who were taking over their country and now, too, their people. It was as though the Indonesians working in the *blanda* homes had become traitors to their own race. It was the start of a slow and dangerous under-current of unrest.

———————

Every morning my father dressed for the tropical climate in shorts, kneesocks, and a short-sleeved shirt, slicking his hair back and brushing it on both sides simultane-ously, with a brush in each hand. Our chauffeur, Ali, then drove him to work. After he left, my mother sat at the dining room table and gave the orders of the day to the head *djongos*. Dressed in a white sari and jacket with a white turban on his head, he stood a respectable distance from the table and listened intently to every word she said. She handed him the menu for the cook and also the money to buy provisions. He was the liaison between the family and the servants in the back. As the head *djongos*, his turban was decorated with a small orange ribbon, a patriotic touch denoting the Dutch House of Orange, or royal family. The other uniforms were plain white.

Our lives were well regulated and very comfortable.

We grew up with opera, especially *Madama Butterfly,* Mozart, Chopin, and my mother's beloved violin music. She herself was quite an accomplished violinist.

Our family shortly after our arrival in Java, 1938. My mother holds me in her arms while my brother, Willem, and my father look on.

Willem and I never ate with our parents except for Sunday breakfast. We were expected to sit up straight with our hands on the table, next to our plates. 'Those are good manners,' my mother said. Grown-ups, we were told, tucked their thumbs inside their curled-up fingers, much like a fist. Occasionally my father's thumb would pop up unexpectedly from its hiding place and he would ceremoniously tuck it back down as though it were misbehaving. He'd look at us and grin, and we would giggle and keep our eyes on his hands, hoping those naughty thumbs would pop out again. My mother would sigh and say, 'Oh, Edu!' and we would try not to laugh too much because we knew we would be sent away from the table.

My parents talked to each other in French when they didn't want us to understand what they were saying. Most of the time we could tell when it was about us, but other times we knew by the way they were laughing and looking at each other that they were sharing a secret meant only for each other.

One morning, my father carefully opened his boiled egg and found a dead baby chick inside. I saw the look that passed between him and my mother, and I also saw the wet little feathers tucked inside the shell before one of the *djongos* whisked the plate away. Not a word was said. One should never make a fuss, we were taught. I strongly believe it was this no-fuss attitude of my mother's that brought us safely through some of the toughest times of our lives.

Sometimes Willem and I were able to slip away from our *baboe* and peek through the door that led into the *djongos'* area, strictly forbidden to us children. The kitchen was here with its wood-burning range, and also the laundry room, where all our clothing was washed by hand. Right inside the door, as we peeked in, stood the table where the silver was polished weekly. Picture frames, platters, and serving dishes. Teapots, milk jugs, and sugar bowls, not to mention all the little teaspoons and assorted cutlery sets. The list went on and on. The *djongos* would sit around this table and polish all day long, so it was really no wonder that their faces lit up when they saw us standing there. Any diversion was welcome.

'Want to see magic?' they said, grinning.

Of course we wanted to see magic, and without a further thought, we stepped right through that forbidden door. They scurried back and forth into the garden, and our excitement rose when the four *djongos* finally settled down, with dishcloths covering their laps, to chant and murmur magic words. Moving their hands up and down under the cloths, they grinned and winked at one another. We were completely under their spell. A few more minutes for effect and then, presto! Out popped a baby bunny from one of the cloths.

Another time it was a little yellow chick. Only our amazement could outshine the joy on their faces that their magic had worked on us again.

Our mother was not quite as excited about this wonderful magic as we were, and would not allow bunnies or chicks to live in our bedroom after she pointed out to us the dreadful consequences all over our floor. After that, our 'magic' animals were all relegated to a coop in the back garden. Sad to say, they did not live harmoniously together for very long. Overcrowding became a problem, and after we had witnessed the decapitation and aimless running in circles of the chicken, we became so upset that any further magic shows were absolutely forbidden.

But there was other magic to be had. Evenings in the soft tropical dusk were always a special time. Bathed and ready for bed, we joined our parents on the veranda while they sipped their sherries and listened to *Aïda* or *The Barber of Seville*. If we were good and sat very still, we could dip one small sugar cube into one of their glasses, then suck it slowly. We would snuggle up close to our mother as she read to us. The best treat was when our father would take us into their darkened bedroom and we'd all huddle on the bed, the four of us, heads together, and watch the sparks fly as he struck two flint stones together. That was magic indeed.

———————

Every day at noon, Ali brought my father back for lunch and a nap. The heat of the day made us all listless and drowsy, as though the world itself slowed and stopped for a few hours. The gorilla in the attic never showed its ugly head during naptime, and we were asleep in no time at all.

Then, in the afternoons, we would either visit friends, take a walk along the tree-lined avenue in front of our house, or go to the local swimming club (Dutch families only) until it was teatime, which we enjoyed outside on the veranda. Willem and I sipped sugared, milky tea from silver mugs inscribed with our names and birth dates. Our mother embroidered while our father read the newspaper. He frowned and read articles about war and invasions out loud. Our mother stopped embroidering and listened intently. She looked at our father with anxious eyes. 'How dreadful! How is that possible?'

Willem and I were sent away to play. Slipping out of the house without our *baboe* noticing, we headed straight to the low stone wall that separated our lawn from the road. We knew that poisonous snakes, cobras mostly, lived in the crevices amid the stones, and we loved to poke long sticks into the holes to make them come out.

Inevitably, one would slither from its hiding place and we would run screaming back to the house. Our screams

Each day we would look forward to teatime in the garden with our mother.

brought all the servants running to our rescue. Our mother, however, did not take kindly to being disturbed. As always, we ended up sitting on straight-backed wooden chairs to reflect upon our bad behavior.

By the next morning, our father would relent and take Willem and me with him to the warehouse, one of our very favorite places.

'Do we get to go to the room with the spices?' we asked. Our eagerness was always rewarded with cinnamon sticks to suck on. After the first sharp taste, they were delicious. Next came the room we were least fond of, the one where the liquid rubber was boiled and made into the large yellow sheets that were then packed for export to England and Europe. The smell was so pungent and sharp, it seemed to burn your nose and throat. The Indonesians did not seem to be affected the same way, and they laughed at us as we covered our noses and held our breath. Then they gave us each a sugarcane. Hard as wood to begin with, the canes softened into a sweet, delicious pulp. The more we chewed, the more juice ran out.

After that, we visited the rubber plantation. The Indonesian men and women tapped the rubber by slicing thin channels in the trees, around and down in a spiral, until the milky liquid ran from a little funnel into a bucket suspended from a nail. From there it would be taken back to the factory, where it was boiled until it thickened, then was poured into large, flat molds until it formed into sheets.

Another day, our father took us to the tea plantations in the hills. We ran laughing between the rows of bushes, watching the nimble fingers of the tea pickers as they plucked the tender leaves and threw them in the tall baskets on their backs. These baskets were suspended by a single leather strap that the women looped around the top of their heads. They were beautiful women in colorful sarongs, with tiny jewels in their noses. On their slender brown arms most of them wore twenty or more very thin, brightly colored glass bangles interspersed with silver ones, which tinkled melodically as they fell together. As the women continued slowly down the rows, they kept up a constant stream of chatter, occasionally shouting to someone farther down the hill and bursting into peals of laughter. No matter how much they talked, they continued to pick at an incredible pace.

Our parents loved Java, and every day our mother tried to show us something new that was beautiful or exciting about the island, from rain forests and rice paddies to volcanoes and jungles where leopards and tigers still roamed. She told us the mythical story of the tiger spirit who looked after the forests, and she walked us through fragile woods where pale moonlight orchids flourished. We stroked the feathery tendrils that hung down from the kapok trees and breathed in the heady fragrances of the honeysuckle vines and lily-of-the-valley flowers that grew among the ferns on the mountain slopes.

She also made sure that we had plenty of time to spend in our own immaculately kept garden with its beautiful flowers, where we could run and play or cool off in the shade of a large litchi tree. My mother had grown to truly love this life.

An overabundance of tropical fruits and vegetables always graced our table. We feasted on litchis, star fruit, papayas, and mangoes throughout each day. Our wonderful servants stood ever ready with their kindly faces to indulge our whims. Full of respect for our parents, they would never step out of line, but Willem and I knew we had them wrapped around our little fingers. We were so sure as children that they would always be there for us whenever we needed them.

3

Echoes of War

In the months that followed, Willem and I sensed a tension in the house. For one thing, our father did not go to the office every day as he used to. Instead, he and our mother spent a lot of time together listening to the news on the radio or reading the newspapers. They whispered softly to each other if they thought we were around. We caught snatches of conversations about war and Japanese soldiers and prisoners. It was obvious that they were trying to keep it all quiet, not realizing that this secrecy just made things more frightening for us. Baboe, too, who seldom showed any emotion, jumped every time she heard a loud noise outside. Several times she burst into tears and rushed from the room.

We were also aware of new and unusual happenings in the neighborhood. Houses were being boarded up; friends suddenly packed all their belongings and left. Occasionally, they simply disappeared overnight. We did not know that these strange happenings were the result of the Japanese attack on Pearl Harbor, halfway across the world. The whole world was now at war, and the Japanese had lost no time in forcing the surrender of the Dutch and British troops on the islands. There was no longer time for escape. Those who did try to flee inevitably lost their lives at sea as their boats were either torpedoed or bombed by the Japanese. Unknown to us then, the Japanese apparently had plans for each and every man living on the islands to work on a railroad to be built through the jungles of Malaysia.

The women were another problem. My mother knew it was just a matter of time until she, like so many women around her, would be forced to leave behind all the objects that she held dear: her house and all its furnishings, her flower gardens, and the faithful *djongos* whom she trusted with her children. She would have to leave the lifestyle she had grown to love so much and knew she would never have again. For as long as she could, however, she tried to ignore the rumors that all women and children were being interned in camps enclosed by barbwire. She had to try and stay out of those camps for as long as possible, because she was pregnant with my brother Gijs, and he was not due for several months yet.

Having just awakened, I lay on my bed staring at the closed curtains, aware that somehow things were very different. I was waiting, but I didn't know for what. There was an eerie silence. Where was the peaceful *scritch-scritch* of gravel? Or the distant voices of the people on the river as they went about their daily business? I was straining my ears for any little noise that could tell me what was happening when I became aware of something else. It was way off in the distance, like the humming of bees. A soft drone that became louder as it neared, until an earsplitting roar overhead made me sit up in bed and scream in terror. Willem bolted out of his bed and rushed over to the window.

'The Japs! The Japs! They are here!' he screamed.

Then total and utter silence. The silence was almost more frightening than the roar of the planes. Timidly, still shaking with fright, I joined him at the window and peered out. Not a soul, not a dog or bird, was to be seen. I glanced at the house across the road. All the windows were tightly closed and shuttered. In my wildly beating heart, I knew that there would be no more singing or wonderful fragrances to enjoy. I somehow felt a kinship with the woman who had lived across the road, even though we had never met and I knew now we never would. I was going to miss her. I was suddenly overcome with sadness and an overwhelming feeling of insecurity, and my thumb shot into my mouth. It was all so bewildering.

We were still at the window trying to understand when our mother came into the room. This in itself was out of the ordinary, but somehow it didn't surprise me. Where was Baboe? She always got us dressed.

'Baboe has gone back to her village to be with her family,' my mother explained. 'I want you to be very good children, and help me as much as you can,' she continued, 'and Claartje' – she turned to me with a serious face – 'I don't want to see you sucking your thumb. You are too big for that now. Besides, it's very dirty.' I put both my hands behind my back and looked at her, shamefaced. She bent down, smiling, and gave me a big hug.

'Look here,' she said. 'I've invented a new game for us to play.' Out of her pocket, she pulled two pieces of cord. She placed one around each of our necks. From the cord hung a small white cotton bag into which a tiny square of that detestable yellow rubber from my father's factory had been sewn. I saw that she was wearing one, too.

'Now, every time you hear those noisy airplanes flying overhead, I want you to pop that little bag into your mouths, between your teeth, like this . . . see . . . and then you must lie facedown on the ground.' She looked at both of us to make sure we were listening. 'We are all going to play this game. No matter where you are, or what you are doing, you must lie down immediately.'

'It's because of the bombs, isn't it?' Willem asked matter-of-factly. 'This way our teeth won't break if a bomb falls too close to us.'

My mother looked at him in surprise and nodded. 'That's right,' she said. 'Just in case.'

At first this game was a lot of fun. We threw ourselves down and looked around to make sure everyone was playing. We giggled to see the *djongos* in their sarongs, arms and legs outstretched, lying with their eyes tightly closed. If Willem and I fell down close together, we yanked on each other's cords to pop the pieces out of our mouths.

But the planes became too numerous and the bombs were falling too close. My father was busy helping the workmen enclose our veranda with large sheets of wood. We no longer had tea out there. Even the windows on the house were boarded up. The house became so dark and dismal that we were forced to keep the lights on all day.

Japanese jeeps and trucks patrolled the avenues on a regular basis, checking for people who were trying for that last-minute escape off the island. Willem and I watched from the doorway until our mother called us back into the house. Somehow we knew that now that the soldiers were here, it would be only a matter of time before they would take over our house, too. So many of our neighbors had already left, taken by those same soldiers 'to a safe location,' they were told, their houses pillaged and their belongings sold on the black market.

It became increasingly unsafe to merely throw yourself to the floor and bite on the rubber piece. Now, as soon as we heard a plane approaching, we had to rush down into the cellar, which had been turned into an air-raid shelter. It smelled disgustingly dank and musty.

An enormous, heavy wooden structure, much like a kitchen table, had been constructed in the middle of the floor by local carpenters. Underneath, several large mattresses lay side by side, and from hooks screwed into the sides of the table, gas masks dangled. One for each member of our household. On top of the table stood huge bottles of drinking water, tins of condensed milk,

Spam, and sardines, and jars of crackers, biscuits, and chocolate bars. A change of clothing for each of us, and assorted books. There were candles and flashlights, matches, and first-aid boxes. One small radio would keep us informed of what was happening in the outside world. In a corner, behind a screen, stood a bucket with a lid. This was the toilet.

The *djongos* refused to come down into the cellar with us. They felt too uncomfortable living so close to the family they worked for. Soon they, too, like our *baboe,* left for their own villages. With tears in their eyes and much bowing and clasping of hands, they promised to return one day and do more magic for us. Perhaps a little kitten or puppy next time? We said we'd like that very much and hoped they'd come back soon. In a few days, maybe?

Ali, the chauffeur, refused to leave. He became our *baboe,* cook, and *djongos* all rolled into one. Being Javanese, he was now the only one among us who could run errands in town. It was no longer safe for us to leave the house. He worked hard to provide us with the best possible meals, but food was becoming scarce in the markets, since the Japanese soldiers always had first choice.

During this time my thumb was always in my mouth

Clara at age four, a few weeks before we were forced to
move into the camps.

I tried to keep it out when my mother was around, but
she always managed to catch me. She tried rubbing bitter
creams on both of my thumbs, but I sucked it right off.
She sewed little cotton bags to slip over my hands, but

I sucked holes right through them. In the end, my father simply said, 'Just let her be.'

Since most of our neighbors were gone, taken by truck into concentration camps, the avenue we lived on was deserted and quiet. The only vehicles that passed were the trucks and jeeps used by the soldiers as they checked daily on those people still living in their own homes. Most nights we now slept under the wooden table in the cellar, for safety. This was becoming more and more difficult for my mother as her pregnancy advanced. My father had to continually help her up and down. Luckily, he stayed home all the time, and he and my mother were never far apart. Their faces were very grim, and their time was spent simply waiting for the inevitable.

Days passed agonizingly slowly, and tensions were becoming almost unbearable when, finally, a knock on the door changed our lives forever.

It was still early in the morning when the loud banging startled us out of a deep sleep. Screams and yells and more heavy pounding sent my father, who was only half dressed, scurrying up the cellar stairs to open the front door.

Two Japanese soldiers with their rifles pointing straight at him, bayonets glistening in the early-morning sun, were standing on the front step. They were screaming in Japanese at the top of their voices, as though they expected my father not to listen. They barked a few instructions in English for him to be ready in one hour, emphasizing their words by shaking their bayonets in his face.

'You hear? One hour! One case only. Don't be late!' Then they swaggered back down the drive. They were in charge now and proud of their new authority.

My mother, her face ashen, was already packing the small case put aside for just this occasion when my father returned. Cotton shirts and shorts, toiletries, a few medical supplies, and a couple of photos. What else would he need? Where was he going?

Ali was hastily dispatched to fetch the Mungers, a Swiss couple who lived at the end of the avenue. 'Call us when you need us,' Mrs. Munger had always said.

Obviously, my father thought it would be a good idea if they came now, when he was leaving. But before Ali could return, the truck that would take my father away from us roared into sight.

He bent down to kiss us hastily. 'Everything is going to be all right,' he whispered. 'Help Mummy with the baby. I'll try to get back as soon as I can.'

No words were spoken between my parents. A few hugs and a kiss, and he hurried down the gravel drive.

The open truck was already full of grim-faced men who pushed one another aside to let him on. He never once looked back as we waved from the doorway. We continued to wave for some time, even when the truck was out of sight.

There was such a feeling of emptiness after our father left that we just wandered around the house aimlessly, Willem and I, touching things we knew we shouldn't touch and wandering into rooms that had always been forbidden. One such room was the servants' quarters. Once our eyes adjusted to the darkness, as there were no windows in this room, we were disappointed to discover that all it contained was a few mattresses on the floor and some pegs on the walls for their sarongs. A little room to the side held a large brick *mandi,* a tub filled with cold water. Nearby hung the dipper for scooping the water to pour over oneself while standing on a slatted wooden platform outside the tub. The water drained away into a hole in the floor. There was no indoor toilet.

Across the hall was another little room. This had been our *baboe*'s room. This room did have a window and even a small mirror on the wall. A mattress on the floor was her bed. As we crept guiltily around the room, we spied a tin with a lid on it at the corner of the mattress. Kneeling down, Willem pried open the lid. He jumped back and gasped as a hairy black ball rolled out onto the floor.

'What is that?' He wrinkled his nose in disgust.

'That's Baboe's hair,' I told him. 'When she brushes her hair and some comes out, she saves it, and then when she wants to have a big bun on her head, she puts this hair on with her other hair.' She had shown me how she did this, many times. Willem looked utterly appalled.

Mrs. Munger was just leaving when we returned from our explorations. We were surprised that we hadn't been missed. We weren't used to such freedom.

The days after our father's departure were spent in the gloom of our boarded-up house. Our mother never let us go outside anymore, and apart from the Mungers, nobody came to visit. Nearly all of our Dutch and British friends had already been taken to concentration camps.

The air in the house became hot and stale as the days passed in aimless waiting. We lay around on our mattresses in the cellar. Our mother read and reread endless storybooks until we knew them by heart. We practiced putting on our gas masks while she timed us. I hated that game.

The mask was so tight around my head, and I couldn't stand the smell of the rubber. Willem growled and advanced menacingly toward me like a ferocious animal until I whipped off his mask and threw it away.

At first our mother would get angry with him for his pranks and make him sit in a corner of the room, but she was tired and looked so sad that she finally stopped making us do anything. Mrs. Munger now came every day to make sure that we were all right.

Life was strange without our father. Every evening we expected him to come whistling in the front door until we remembered that he was not coming home. We wondered where he was and what he was doing.

The days became very long. Down in the cellar, lit only by electric lights, the dark days rolled into dark nights. Outside, the planes continued to roar overhead, and from time to time we felt the deep rumble or shaking of the earth as a bomb dropped elsewhere on the island.

My mother had taken to sleeping on top of the table, as she could no longer get up once she was down on the floor. The baby was due any day now. Willem and I didn't really know what this meant. We knew we were going to get a new little sister or brother, but from where, we didn't know. Since we never left the house anymore, maybe Ali would bring one home for us — sort of like the magic the *djongos* would perform.

In my mind, however, there was nothing particularly magical about the day my little brother arrived. It was August 20, 1942. A faint light shone down into the cellar from the open door upstairs. This in itself was foreboding. That door was always closed. Crawling out from under the table, we saw that our mother was not in her bed on top. We ventured to the stairs and stood still to listen. Not a sound from anywhere.

With anxiously beating hearts, we crept up the stairs and looked about. The tightly shuttered house was dark and gloomy. The stone floors were cold on our bare feet. Standing close to my brother's side, I had never felt as alone as I did then. My thumb left my mouth just long enough for me to scream 'Mummy' into the emptiness. Willem looked at me with terror.

A muffled response came from the living room. Not our mother's voice.

'In here, children.'

Then rustlings and shuffles of slippers across the floor. We stood rooted to the spot. A disheveled Mrs. Munger appeared, running her fingers through her hair and straightening her rumpled skirt. We peered behind her in hopes that our mother was there, too.

'You have a dear little brother now,' Mrs. Munger told us. 'He was born last night in the hospital, and your mummy said you can come to see him.'

We drove to the hospital in Mrs. Munger's car. It was strange to be going out again after being restricted like prisoners all this time. She said it was safe, that the soldiers wouldn't stop us because she and Mr. Munger were Swiss and therefore not in the war.

All the houses we passed were boarded up like ours. In homes where we had played many times, the families were long gone, most of them already taken prisoner.

I was surprised to see the *sate* vendor still hunched over his coal fire at the end of our avenue. My mouth watered as I remembered the one time I was allowed to go with Baboe to buy one small stick of roasted pork balls rolled in peanut-butter sauce from this old man.

All along the route to the hospital we passed Japanese soldiers, trucks, tanks, and jeeps. Rickshas were loaded high with chairs and tables, boxes, and big round bundles of knotted blankets containing clothes, pillows, and other items plundered from abandoned homes. We were so totally absorbed by all the activity outside the car windows, as it had been such a long time since we'd been out of the house, that we had almost forgotten where we were going until Mrs. Munger urged us to get out.

'It's all right,' she said. 'You can get out here. Your mother is waiting for you.' We had arrived at the hospital.

She led us down a long white corridor with many fans whirring in the ceilings, and into a room filled with dozens of beds. To our surprise, each bed had a woman sitting or lying down in it. Where was our mother? Where was our new brother?

Mrs. Munger led us halfway across the room to a bed decorated with brightly colored balloons. Our mother was sitting there with a ribbon tied in her hair. She was smiling and held out her arms. We were so relieved to see her.

I scanned the bed for the baby. I even picked up the edge of the sheet and peered into the bed. To my surprise, I saw that our mother was sitting on a round, doughnut-shaped pillow. I hastily dropped the sheet back in place just as a nurse arrived who offered to take us to see the baby. Her long white starched uniform rustled and crackled as she sped down the corridor. Willem and I had to run to keep up with her. We were not prepared for the next surprise. On entering the nursery, all we could see were rows upon rows of white metal cribs. In each crib lay a sleeping baby all rolled up in a white blanket. Just a little head peeked out of the top. Were all these babies ours? I'd never seen so many babies. The nurse assured us that only one of them was our new little brother. But how did she know which one?

As she led us past the rows of cribs, I tried to peek into each one. I was not at all convinced that the nurse would be able to find the correct baby. Most of the babies had jet-black hair and brown faces. They all looked incredibly alike. Then she stopped at a crib where a very pink baby without any hair lay sleeping.

'This is your little brother, Gijs,' she told us proudly, as though she had made him herself. How could she be so sure? I continued to look into the other cribs. Just in case.

———

That trip to the hospital was to be the last time that we would leave the house in a civilian car.

Gijs was only a few weeks old when Ali came rushing, hot and flustered, into the house one day. It was obvious that he had been running quite a distance.

'Oh! I'm so sorry,' he said, panting. He was almost crying. 'Not my fault, though. Jap soldiers took the car. I'm so sorry.'

He shook his head and wrung his hands as he paced back and forth. My mother made him sit down and tried to calm him. It appeared that he had gone into town to fetch some groceries and had become aware of several Japanese soldiers following him. After he had deposited his groceries in the trunk of the car, one of the soldiers walked up to him and demanded the keys.

'Official business,' they told him.

Several soldiers then climbed into the backseat and, without further explanation, drove away, leaving Ali to walk the several miles home.

'It's all right, Ali, it's not your fault,' my mother said quietly. 'You know they've done this to everyone around here. It was going to happen sooner or later.'

But the stress of it all was too much for Ali. He felt he had let us down badly, and not long after the soldiers took our Buick, he left to go live with his own people. We were now alone. My mother knew that our time was up.

It was therefore no surprise when, one sultry evening, an officer of the Imperial Japanese Army came shuffling up the gravel driveway. My mother waited for him to bang on the front door. It seemed they had never learned to use doorbells. He was carrying a ripped cardboard box that he handed over to her with a smirk on his face.

'In payment for car. Japanese very honorable.'

My mother never said a word, just stared into the box. The smell alone should have warned her. An oozing, yellow mound crawling with hundreds of white maggots lay in the box. It had once been cheese. The soldier then took a slip of paper from his pocket. Even before he could read it, she knew it was the notice to pack up and leave. We had two days. We could take only what we could carry and a couple of mattresses.

'Be ready! Don't bring too much! No weapons! No radios! No cameras!' We would be taken to a safe place to live. We must obey! By order of the Imperial Japanese Army.

4

Preparing to Enter Camp,
September 1942

My mother seemed almost relieved that our time had finally come. No more waiting. No more worrying about that knock on the door that would signal the end of our freedom. Our food was running low, and it was no longer safe to venture from home.

The Japanese soldiers patrolling the avenues in their jeeps were now on foot, day and night. Sometimes one would stand right at the end of our driveway, watching the house. My mother would get nervous and make sure that all the doors were securely locked. She'd send us down to play in the cellar, telling us to stay very quiet. All the while, she kept checking through a small hole in one of the shutters and wouldn't relax until she was sure that the soldier had gone away. There had been so many break-ins at homes all around us that my mother was constantly on edge. These soldiers were known to brutally force their way in and help themselves to everything you owned. If you got in their way, they beat you.

She desperately tried to avoid such a confrontation, feeling so vulnerable with three small children. Since my brother Gijs's birth, she slept under the table with us again, and kept a *knuppel,* a billy club, right next to her side of the mattress. Gijs slept in a basket between us. He was now six weeks old.

The two days that followed the order for us to prepare for camp were hectic. Making the right decisions about what to bring with us seemed to overwhelm my mother at first. The comfort or misery of our life in prison camp depended a great deal on the items she chose to pack. But where to start?

To begin with, she dragged out two of the largest suitcases she could find and opened them in the middle of the floor. Then she walked around the house opening every cupboard and chest of drawers and leaving them ajar. She pulled out dresses and shoes, hats and pretty nightgowns. The pile on her bed was impressive. Then

My mother (seated on table), with her sisters and my grandmother, in India, 1921.

she did the same in our room. By the time she got to the baby's things, she realized that there was no chance everything would fit in the two suitcases. And she hadn't even started on the other necessities yet. Towels, sheets, toiletries, and eating utensils. She sat down on the floor next to the suitcases and burst into tears.

Willem and I crouched beside her and stared at her face. We didn't say a word. This was something new to us. Our mother was always the one in control. It was important to her that things were done correctly. There was a right way and a wrong way. She had grown up in a home with servants where things were always done for her. When she married my father, she had every reason to expect that way of life would continue.

Her younger years were spent in India, where her father worked as supervisor and quality controller on the large sugar plantations. She was the youngest daughter, with two older sisters and a younger brother. A musically gifted child, she wished for nothing more than to be able to play her beloved violin, something her parents tried hard to discourage her from doing. 'There are more worthy pastimes a girl could occupy herself with.'

But my mother was persistent and managed to persuade her parents to provide lessons. Though she became quite an accomplished violinist, they never took her playing seriously.

'Just a passing phase,' they would say.

When the family returned to Holland from India, my

mother was enrolled in an agricultural college in Swansea, Wales. Since she loved gardening and animals so much, her parents considered the college an excellent diversion. It was during one of her vacations in Holland that she met her future husband, Edu.

'Such a respectable young man!' The family sighed with relief. Good family, excellent prospects, and well traveled. He had joined his father's export-import firm and would eventually manage the business in Java. Everyone was happy. She was going to continue in the lifestyle to which she was accustomed.

Now here she was, twenty-nine years old and alone in a boarded-up house with three small children. A husband, who knew where? No chauffeur, no cook, no *baboe,* and worst of all, no one to help her pack. Where to start? What would we need? She looked up and saw us still sitting there, staring at her.

'Well!' she said. 'I think we'd better get on, don't you?'

She jumped up and returned everything to the cupboards. What did we really need? Clothes, definitely, but how long would we be prisoners? Little children outgrew clothes so fast, how many could she possibly pack? She paced the floor and looked around the room.

She had an idea. She opened the linen closet and methodically sorted through the impeccably ironed and starched sheets and tablecloths. She took out several piles of each and laid them neatly in one of the suitcases. These would be good to make into clothes if that ever became necessary. Next came towels, soaps, and eating utensils. Some cups and plates were pushed between the linens so they wouldn't break. Needles, thread, scissors. Rope, paper, pencils, and crayons. A few medical supplies, although surely there would be doctors wherever we were going, and all the bottles of cod-liver oil that she had so carefully saved over the past few months. Every corner, nook, or cranny held a small bottle. She could never have realized at that time that the cod-liver oil would turn out to be the most precious commodity she had brought. Next came buttons, several rolls of string, and a small box of pins. Baby clothes and milk powder. A few light cotton dresses for herself and several changes of clothes for Willem and me.

The suitcases were full to bursting, but we had to find room for our Children's Bible, with its beautiful pictures. My mother considered this Bible a wonderful book, as it contained stories to interest each of us. Positive stories in which good always triumphed over evil. Incredible stories, like the parting of the seas or Jesus walking on the water. In our eyes he could do anything. She had only recently started reading to us the chapters she thought we would understand. The birth of the baby in a stable surrounded by farm animals. Noah's ark filled with wild animals caught in a torrential flood and Jesus filling the fishermen's nets with so many fish, they could hardly haul them out of the sea. She hoped that some of the stories would help us to get through the more difficult times ahead. If we got to the end of the book, she could simply turn back to the beginning and start all over again. Who knew, maybe we would be home again before that happened.

And now she was done. Tomorrow the truck would arrive, and our new life would begin. She wandered around the house studying the paintings on the walls and the photos in their silver frames, smiling wistfully as she remembered the happier times they portrayed. How quickly things had changed.

She tucked her precious violin in the far back of her clothes cupboard and pulled several of her evening gowns to the front, hiding it. Useless, really, as she knew her home would be overrun and ransacked as mercilessly as all the other houses in the neighborhood had been.

Finally, she dragged a couple of mattresses to the front door and stood them on their sides, wrapping several sheets around them so they wouldn't get dirty.

One suitcase was already closed and stood next to the mattresses. It was almost too heavy for her to lift. The second one she left open in case she thought of any last-minute additions.

Willem and I had to pick up our toys and arrange them on our shelves. The dishes, too, were neatly stored in their cupboards, and the tables were cleared. We pretended we were leaving for a trip, a vacation, and would be returning soon.

That night, instead of going down into the cellar, we slept in our own beds for the very last time. I wondered what would become of the gorilla when we were gone.

'Will Pappie be able to find us?' I asked our mother as she bent to tuck us in.

'Of course he will,' she answered. 'He'll come to get us and take us all back to Holland one day.' It already seemed so long since our father had left. We didn't even know where he was.

We were ready and waiting when we heard the dreaded honking of the truck out in the road. Our mother opened the door and signaled that we were coming. She had thought of one last item that she definitely wanted to take with her. Putting baby Gijs down on the Oriental carpet in the hall, she dashed back into the living room and returned clutching her favorite painting, *The Flamboya Tree*. Turning it over, she quickly removed it from its large, ornate frame and tucked it carefully among the sheets and tablecloths. She had fallen in love with this painting the first time she saw it in a small gallery in Ceylon. As a young bride in a faraway country, she was trying to make her new house more like a home. There was something about the way the tree's graceful trunk arched out and over to shade the sandy path below with a crown of vibrant pink and scarlet blossoms that made her want to linger in its shadows. She had seen flamboya trees and was always amazed that something so beautiful and delicate could thrive in such intense heat and humidity. The painting filled her with a sense of peace. She was glad that she had remembered it. Over the next few years, that painting, suspended from a thin cloth cord, became the symbol of home for us. We lived wherever it was hung.

Outside, the honking became urgent and demanding. Two Japanese soldiers strode up the drive, their heavy boots crunching the gravel. They waved their arms, shouting, *'Lekas! Lekas!'* Hurry! Hurry! Didn't we know we shouldn't keep the Imperial Army waiting?

My mother struggled with the suitcases and the baby

in her arms. She was slow. She was wasting the Imperial Army's time. And the soldiers were becoming impatient. The open truck was already full of other women and children, none of whom we knew, sitting in the broiling sun. Several of the women jumped down and offered to help. They dragged the mattresses into the truck, then came back for the suitcases. The soldiers stood by with their rifles raised, shouting abuse, never lifting a finger to help. My mother turned back to lock the door when one of the soldiers jabbed her side with his bayonet.

'Get back!' he screamed. He was becoming hysterical. 'Get in truck. No need to lock door. Not your house now.' He placed himself between us and the house, legs apart and rifle pointing.

Pushing us ahead, she hurried down the drive. Arms reached down to pull us up into the open truck. There was very little space, and we clambered over the many suitcases and mattresses piled on the truck floor. Women moved over to make room for our mother, who sat with Gijs on her lap. Nobody said a word as the truck roared off. A few more stops, a few more families, and the truck was more than full.

We traveled all day in the oppressive heat of a blazing sun. There was no shade on the truck, and the heat was heightened by closely packed bodies. The dry dust, churned up by the wheels, came up and over us in great brown swirls, sticking to our sweaty faces and arms until we felt we would choke on it. Our throats were parched, but there were no stops for food or water. We had wasted enough time by being so slow. Most of the children were crying and begging to go home. People were grabbing at anything that might provide at least a little shade, sharing straw hats with those who, like us, had forgotten to bring theirs.

We had become part of a long caravan of trucks, all traveling from Bandung to Batavia. All moving slowly through tiny, squalid *kampongs,* villages, where people rushed out of their homes to see us pass. Many tried to hand up containers of water but were cruelly pushed away by the Japanese guards. The mothers on the trucks were begging for the water for the children but were denied even that.

'Later,' they were told.

Overheated, exhausted, dirty, and extremely dehydrated, we finally arrived at the entrance gates to Kamp Tjideng. When the gates closed behind us, even we children knew our lives would never be the same.

5

Entry into Kamp Tjideng

As we rode into the compound, we all craned our necks to get our first look at this place they called a concentration camp. For all intents and purposes, it looked much like the small towns we had come from, streets and avenues lined with family homes and gardens. There was one big difference: The whole town was enclosed by a high fence of thick barbwire.

My mother really didn't know what to expect, but she hoped she would get a nice little house where she would be safe with her children. She began to wonder if she had brought the correct supplies to make life comfortable, but they would just have to do. She might have to buy some things at the store. She had brought some money, thank goodness, so for now, she just sat back and surveyed the scene. A large crowd had gathered along the roadway, waiting quietly for the trucks. She scanned the faces of the women but did not recognize anyone. Wouldn't it be comforting, she thought, if some of her friends were here.

The trucks slowly inched their way into the camp. The crowd of women who had been waiting so patiently suddenly surged forward en masse and surrounded the trucks. The guards had a hard time keeping control of them as they shouted and waved at the newcomers. Everyone was anxious to find relatives or friends who might be on the trucks.

My baby brother lay sleeping on my mother's lap. He was lightly covered with a little sheet to protect him from the sun and dust, while Willem and I sat squeezed next to her on the metal seat. We were looking around, trying to take it all in. It was so hot in the blazing sun that the perspiration rolled down our grimy faces as our truck moved slowly through the crowd. The throng milling around was making it almost impossible to advance when a woman in the crowd pushed forward, waving both arms. 'Claar!' she shouted. 'Claar!'

My mother saw her immediately and leaned out over

the side. 'Bep! My God, what a blessing.' She couldn't believe that one of her dearest friends was here. They held tightly on to each other's hands, not wanting to let go as the truck lurched slowly on.

'I'm in block four,' Bep told my mother. 'Give me the baby. I'll find you when you are settled.'

My mother handed Gijs over to her just as a Japanese officer pulled Bep roughly away from the truck. I was overcome with fear for my little brother. How would we ever find Gijs again among all these people? Already I could no longer see him through the waving arms.

The truck stopped and started and stopped again. Mothers and children climbed down with all their belongings when their names were called at each stop. This gave my mother a good chance to see what kind of housing we were getting. She was becoming fully aware of the neglected gardens without flowers and the parched lawns. What was even more upsetting to her was the number of people who seemed to be living in each house. Could that be possible? With a heart growing heavier by the minute, she scrutinized the houses that were still ahead of us as we continued our slow journey. This was certainly not the kind of home she had anticipated.

When the truck finally stopped again, an officer asked

my mother her name. Clara Olink. He checked the long list he was carrying and told her, 'Block one. *Garage.*' She gasped as she heard the words and did not move.

It was the officer's high-pitched voice, ordering her off the truck with her bundles, that brought her back to reality. The realization that we were now totally at the mercy of the Japanese was very frightening. Better to make the best of it, she thought, and concentrate on surviving. She would try to do as she was told and stay out of their way as much as she could. She also knew now that there wouldn't be a store where she could buy things to make life easier. The situation was worse than she had imagined. Hopefully, she had packed everything we would need.

And so it was that we walked slowly and sadly into the garage, pulling our suitcases behind us. It was damp and extremely dirty.

'Why don't we go into the house, Mummy?' we asked her.

'Because that is already full of people,' she answered in a matter-of-fact manner. We looked up at the many curious faces staring at us from the windows. Nobody said a word.

We walked all the way to the back of the garage. In one of the side walls a hole had been hacked, big enough to serve as a door. It looked out over a small backyard and also provided the only light.

'We'll have this end, children. This will make a nice little room for us. Put your things down so people will know this space is ours.'

We looked around and held on to our parcels. We didn't want this to be ours. It was filthy, and there wasn't anywhere to sit down.

While Willem and I stood in the middle of the garage in complete silence, our mother strung some of the rope she had packed high across the garage, from one side wall to the opposite wall, incorporating the gap as our door. Then she disappeared to borrow a broom. I felt forlorn, thirsty, and ready to cry. When I looked at our mattresses lying outside in the dirt, tears started to flow and my thumb went into my mouth. Couldn't we just go home?

Two more families arrived, weary mothers dragging children and trunks into the garage. They eyed our corner with envy and tried to push into our space. But our mother had hung several sheets down to the floor and pinned them in place, so we had a wall, though the width of our space was the length of our mattress.

Willem and I watched her every move from our spot on the mattress. She had laid both mattresses on the cement floor, one on top of the other, against the wall opposite our 'door.' In the little backyard she found an abandoned chest of drawers that she dragged inside, too. After cleaning out the bottom drawer, she lined it with towels and baby blankets as a crib for Gijs. The other drawers she filled with our eating utensils, dishes, and household items. Our clothes and linens and all the bottles of cod-liver oil were left in the suitcases for now. She then placed Gijs's drawer on top of the cases, off the floor. Last but not least, she hung the painting of the flamboya tree on the rear wall. This crude room was now our home.

Next we all went in search of the bathroom and toilet. The bathroom was already taken over by a young family who had simply thrown all their belongings into the tub and arranged their mattresses around it. When we looked in, they explained that there was no running water anyway. Before we even opened the door to the toilet next door, we could smell what we were going to find. The toilet was blocked and had overflowed onto the floor. Maggots and flies crawled over the mess on the floor and up the walls as we backed away in disgust.

Holding our noses, Willem and I hurried after our

mother as she peeked into the various rooms of the house. It was filled to capacity with other mothers and children. There was very little furniture; mattresses covered most of the floor space. Here and there people were using their trunks and suitcases as cupboards and tables. It was so crowded that we rushed to get out of there.

'Aren't we lucky to have our own little room?' our mother said, seizing the opportunity to point out to us that the garage wasn't such a bad place after all. Strangely enough, we began to feel better.

The other families who joined us in the garage took some time to get settled in, as they were still arguing about which space each was entitled to. By now it was late afternoon, and we still hadn't eaten anything. From somewhere, my mother acquired both a potty and a bucket for water. We were told that the only source of water was from the tap at the side of the driveway, near the road. And the only place to dump the potty was directly into the sewer in the road, after lifting the manhole cover. Unfortunately, we never had enough water to rinse the potty.

Japanese soldiers were everywhere, patrolling the streets, trying to keep order, especially where people were still fighting over living spaces. Tensions were high, and the late-afternoon heat unbearable. All the newly arrived prisoners were exhausted and extremely hungry. We had had nothing to eat or drink since leaving our home in the early morning, so my mother approached one of the guards and asked when the next meal would arrive, or where she could get something for the children. Surely we would get food and water? The guard eyed her angrily and pointed at the tap beside the road.

'There. There water. You drink water. Food tomorrow. Too late food today.' He screamed the words at her.

Luckily, she had packed a few items of food, tins mostly, but we were almost too tired to eat. Willem and I were already asleep by the time Bep brought Gijs to the garage. She and my mother were just settling down to speak when a loud ruckus in the street startled us all. An officer sitting in the back of a jeep was screaming through a bullhorn that everyone was to gather immediately in front of their houses, in neat orderly lines, to be welcomed by the commandant.

'*Lekas!*' Hurry!

We soon learned that the Japanese officers were unable to speak in normal tones. Every word was screamed in angry commands and always followed by '*Lekas! Lekas!*'

Confusion reigned in the street by the time we got there. A few lines were forming, mostly by the prisoners who had been in camp for a while. The new arrivals, like us, had no idea what was expected, but we were going to learn in a hurry. We stood around in tired, hungry groups. Gijs was screaming, and Willem and I clung to our mother, begging to go back to sleep. The guards were rushing up and down the lines, slapping and pushing people into the spots where they were supposed to stand. They wanted straight lines, facing into the road, with a space big enough for an officer to walk between for inspection. We were each numbered, so many from the front, so many from the back. Always the same line. Always the same spot. Always the same number. Straight lines. Silent lines. No talking. Ever!

Willem and I were in the row to the left of my mother, one behind the other. This way she still had eye contact with us. It was absolutely forbidden to touch or talk or to make contact in any way with another person in line. You could never turn around or sit down, no matter how tired you were. And always, in order to show respect, you had to bow when confronted by a Japanese officer, head lowered, arms down by your side, and leaning forward at the waist. At roll call, the command would be given to bow: *'Keirei!'* We were to stay in this position until told to straighten. *'Naore!'* Anybody not bowing correctly, or rising before being told to do so, could expect to be beaten with the butt of a rifle, kicked in the ribs, or left standing in the sun for the remainder of the day.

Tenkos, roll calls, were for counting heads. But, being easily distracted by a person out of line or looking at him the wrong way, an officer would often lose count, and the whole process would have to start anew. The lines stretched across the road from one sidewalk to the other. All prisoners stood in the section of road directly outside their own house, with everyone facing the same direction. This meant that some prisoners stood with their backs to their houses, as there were houses on both sides of the road. To begin with, there were fifty to sixty people living in a single home, so the lines were fairly well spaced. As the war progressed, however, and the commandant realized how stressful and unbearable he could make the situation by cramming more and more people together, the numbers grew to several hundred in each home. This made counting of heads much more difficult for the guards. Sometimes we were expected to hold the bowed position so long that we either fell over or had to steady ourselves by leaning our hands on our knees. On days when we were out in the blazing sun for hours on end, without water or shade, many people simply crumbled to the ground and lay there unconscious until the lines were dismissed and someone could come to their aid with water.

We had a lot to learn, it seemed, but the officers were going to teach us.

For now, the lines were straight, we had almost mastered the bow, and the commandant was on his way. He was a squat little man dressed in an immaculately pressed khaki uniform that made him look even rounder and shorter because of the big balloonlike 'wings' that stuck out from his trousers at the thighs. He wore a peaked cap that shaded his face. His knee-high black boots, polished to a shine, had hard soles that were loud and impressive as he marched up and down the sidewalks in front of the lines.

How we learned to fear and hate the sound of those boots! Soldiers with bayonets on their rifles walked closely behind him, always at the ready for the command to reprimand a difficult prisoner.

Today the commandant told everyone assembled in the road how very lucky we were to be here. We were safe. We would be well taken care of. We must obey and work hard. We must not waste water or food. We *must* respect.

Again we bowed, then stayed in that position until he had jumped in his jeep to be driven to the next road where the same speech would be delivered. We were ordered back to our quarters to settle down for the night. There was to be total silence.

'Lekas!' Hurry!

That night, my mother started reading to us from the Children's Bible. She would continue to do this for the next three and a half years, by which time we would know every word by heart.

6

Life in Camp

It did not take us long to settle into the routine of camp life, once we had mastered the rules in order of importance. The first and foremost lesson was that the Japanese were now in charge. Every order or command was intended to reinforce the message that prisoners must obey without question anything the officers demanded of us. Another rule, as important to the Japanese as obedience, was respect. The way to show respect was to bow every time your paths crossed. It was so important to them, in fact, that failure to bow was reason enough for punishment. It didn't matter what you were doing, be it riding a bike or carrying a vat of boiling water, the rules demanded that you get off the bike or put down the boiling water to immediately pay your respects. Many unfortunates were beaten severely with fists in their faces before they realized what was expected of them.

My mother had made up her mind early on that we would avoid confrontation by staying out of their way and complying with their rules. She had three young children and could not afford to endanger her life or ours.

Each day we were awakened by the wailing of sirens summoning us all into the streets for *tenko,* roll call. Most of the time it was simply to count heads. Did they really believe someone could have escaped during the night? A lot of natives outside the barbwire fence were as hostile to us as the Japanese soldiers inside; they still harbored a lot of anger and resentment that we had so successfully taken over their island and, in a lot of instances, their people. Now that all the *blandas,* whites, were incarcerated, small bands of rebels were already forming who hoped to overthrow the Dutch government eventually. They definitely did not want us on their side of the barbwire, and we knew perfectly well that they would not help us in any way. Death would be the ultimate punishment if we were caught trying to escape.

Often we were summoned at an unexpected time

because of rumors that a radio, newspapers, or weapons were hidden somewhere in the camp. These rumors caused such anxiety among the guards that they would stop at nothing until they had found the forbidden articles. Summoned out at a moment's notice, we would not have time to hide anything or, for that matter, have time to eat or drink, which reinforced their power over us.

Soon after our arrival, we stood in long lines in the merciless sun for hours on end while the guards tore apart every single item we owned. They trampled the precious, meager rations of rice we had saved from the day before, then smashed all our dishes. After our dishes and cups were destroyed, we had to use tin lids for plates and empty Spam containers for cups.

Until the guards had finished with these searches, we did not dare to move from our spots in line. Even bathroom needs were ignored. People who sat down from sheer fatigue would be slapped and kicked so hard that standing again became virtually impossible.

The raids could last all day and well into the night if nothing was found. And all that time we stood. Almost the worst part about the raids was missing a whole day of food rations, as the women who cooked the food were also in line. At those times, we drank a lot of water when we returned to our quarters, and saved our energy by lying around on our mattress. Sleep is difficult to achieve, though, when your stomach is cramping and all you can think of is food. We'd toss and turn and listen to the desperate crying, all night long, of those whose hunger pains were more than they could bear.

Tenko was more than just a time to count heads and search rooms. It was also a time for breaking our spirits, teaching us humility, and showing us how worthless we were. As soon as the Japanese realized that they were up against some tough opposition with the women in this camp, who were not going to give in that easily, they devised more and more methods of bringing everyone down to their knees. Prisoners who were too sick or weak from starvation and could not make it out to their spot in line were dragged from their mattresses and dumped in the road. Here they were forced to lie in the full sun for several hours, where many of them perished. Others, by now severely sunburned and dehydrated, would be gently lifted and carried back inside by their friends at the end of *tenko*.

———

My mother felt lucky that the guards confined their searches to the personal items each prisoner had brought into camp, such as mattresses, suitcases, and clothes, because quite accidentally she had become the nervous owner of a very large, and very sharp, dagger.

She and I had been hanging some wash on a line in the little back garden adjacent to our garage when she tripped over something sticking up out of the ground. Not wanting anyone else to trip over it, too, she grabbed hold of the offending article and pulled. Once she had loosened it, it slipped easily out of the ground. To her utmost horror, she saw that she was holding a perfectly good dagger in her hands. 'Oh my God, now I'm in trouble,' she whispered breathlessly as she stared at the shiny blade. With her heart pounding, she glanced nervously around to see whether anyone besides me had been watching. Then, tucking it quickly under her blouse, she rushed back inside.

What was she going to do with it? I wondered. The guards would never believe she had found it. But where had it come from? She could already picture herself forced to kneel in front of a guard as he hacked viciously at her hair with the dagger until she was bald. She knew this was one of their favorite punishments. She would have a lot of explaining to do, and they were not going to listen to her.

'Calm down! Think! Think! Think!' she kept telling

herself as she paced anxiously back and forth, still clutching the dagger underneath her blouse. She realized suddenly that there was only one thing she *could* do. Going outside again, she hastily stuck the dagger back into the ground and then tied the end of the wash line to its handle, to make it look as though it was the steadying post to which the line was attached. She took a few steps back and breathed deeply. She felt relieved that it looked so good. Once she calmed down, she had to admit to herself that it was also a rather comforting feeling, knowing she had such a big knife in case of emergencies. Happily, she never had to use it to defend herself, and when we were moved to a different location, she left it holding up the wash line.

Every day in camp was much like the day before. Time passed with painful slowness. We were always glad if there hadn't been too much trouble with the guards. No unexpected beatings or long *tenkos* in the sun. Over time, it was the small events, such as the arrival of the rice, that became the highlight of our days. The big vats of rice, carried by two women, usually arrived in the late morning and were left on a table at the end of the driveway. This was our food station, where a designated leader from the house doled out the food by the spoonful. So many spoons per person, per day. It worked out to about one small bowl each. In the beginning, we could also expect a small serving of bean shoots, a package of tea leaves, and occasionally a loaf of hard black bread. The only thing you could do with the bread to make it edible was dunk it in the tea. My mother would often make soup out of the tea by adding salt, which she scraped from a large salt brick of the type usually given to cows to lick. Every prisoner had been given one. Tea soup was a wonderful addition to our meals, as it managed to make us feel full.

The tea leaves served other useful purposes. Not only were they able to disguise the terrible color and taste of the drinking water, but they also contained many healing properties. A compress made of hot tea leaves strapped around a boil or infected wound was excellent for drawing out the poisons. When my mother spilled boiling water on her arm, she walked around for a week with it bandaged with tea leaves. Although severely burned, her arm never became infected. Unfortunately, as the war dragged on, the bread, bean shoots, and precious tea leaves were taken from us. We were 'unworthy people' who did not deserve special considerations.

We collected our rice in a round black pan with a lid.

The rice would still be fairly warm, so my mother would sit it in the middle of the mattress and cover it completely with pillows and towels. This way it might stay warm until the next meal. Before she covered it, she would allow us to pick out one lump of rice each as a special treat. The bread, when we had it, was something we could set aside until later. When food became something you couldn't rely on receiving every day, it was wise to keep a loaf well hidden, for emergencies. But no matter how carefully you tried to hide it, it was something that could be stolen, and often was. It caused many fights and intense feelings of mistrust. It also attracted rats, which would walk over our faces as we slept. Even when a rat chewed on your small loaf, you didn't throw it out. You simply scraped away his tooth marks and ate the bread before he came back for more.

Our days came to revolve more and more around food — its arrival or its consumption. My mother had acquired a skill for making these rudimentary meals satisfying and fulfilling. We didn't need to be told twice to get ready for a meal, as mealtime came around only too slowly. We watched intently as she dished up. Spreading one scoop of rice onto our tin plates, she spread it around so it covered the whole plate. It looked like more that way. We didn't start eating until everyone was served, and then we ate slowly, savoring every bite. It was not important who finished first. In fact, it seemed more important to finish last.

Even here in the camp, my mother was strict about manners. At the end of each meal, she insisted we sit quietly and wait until every member of the family had finished eating. Then, with a nod, she allowed us to pick up our plates and lick them clean. She did the same with her plate, until not a morsel was left to be washed off. This certainly made dishwashing much easier, as we had little water and no soap, and often resorted to sand when a scrub was needed. A lot of people frowned on the habit of plate licking. 'Animals lick plates,' they said scornfully. '*We'll* never stoop so low.' My mother refused to be cowed by such talk.

'It tastes mighty good to me,' she answered. 'You should consider yourselves lucky that you have food to waste.'

She encountered a lot of resentment in her daily interactions with other women, especially married women without children. 'You're so lucky,' they told her. 'I miss my husband so much. Oh God, I wish he was here.'

'Wouldn't that be *wonderful!*' my mother agreed.

'You have nothing to complain about,' they said. 'At least you have children.'

'That doesn't mean I don't miss my husband,' she'd answer.

One day a special treat was announced for the prisoners. Pudding! We were going to have dessert! As soon as the rice arrived, we all swarmed around the food table. We wanted to see for ourselves if it was true. Indeed, there was the pan with the rice and, wonder of wonders, in tin containers right next to it, the dessert. We could smell the rice, but no matter how hard we sniffed, we were unable to catch the aroma of the pudding. Very carefully we carried the treasure back to our quarters. Mother placed it in the middle of the crate table and we all gathered around it, to stare and sniff and shake the container. It was gray and jellylike, had no delicious odor, and didn't really move when you shook the tin.

'I have an idea,' our mother said. 'Tomorrow is my birthday. Why don't we keep this pudding until then as a special treat?'

We were dreadfully disappointed, and I started to cry, but birthdays were still important, and since we couldn't expect gifts, we had to make the day special with whatever means we had.

We returned to the dessert pan repeatedly to stare at

its contents. By evening, the gray mass shook and wobbled slightly when touched. Our mother finally covered it with a cloth because we couldn't be trusted to leave it alone.

The next day seemed to take forever, but finally the time for dessert did come. We sang 'Happy Birthday' with great enthusiasm, all the while keeping our eyes on that covered tin with the mouthwatering dessert. There lay that gray mass, more glistening and shiny than we remembered. Our mother stuck in the spoon and scooped. The solid gray mass was no more. It slid off the spoon in sparkling dollops. We couldn't believe what we were seeing. Our mother bent down and sniffed at the pan. 'What's the matter, Mum?' we inquired anxiously. She was not smiling, and we sensed that something was wrong. We watched closely as she took a little of the gray jelly between her fingers and rubbed them together. Carefully she placed a bit on her tongue and tasted it. Dashing across the room, she hastily spat out the door.

'Oh, my darlings,' she whispered to us, 'there is no pudding after all. This is starch. Clothes starch!' There were tears in her eyes as she looked at each of us in turn. 'They tried to trick us,' she said sadly, her shoulders slumping as she tried to hide her anger at this cruelty.

Slowly, Willem got up from the floor. 'We should have

eaten it yesterday' was all he said as he walked angrily away from the table. Our mother watched him go, biting her lips. Willem was always so hungry.

––––––––––

The concentration camp was surrounded by an eight-foot-high barbwire fence. The wires were strung close together to deter any attempts at escape, but even so, Japanese soldiers patrolled along the outside. At first we were able to stand and watch the Javanese natives as they went about their daily activities outside the camp, but this annoyed them so much that they started to hurl stones and bamboo spears through the fence at anybody they caught watching. It became such a problem that *gedek,* bamboo matting, was put up against the barbwire, preventing us from looking out and the Javanese from looking in. There was an advantage to this matting. Now that the guards felt they didn't have to patrol so diligently, we had more opportunities to trade goods with those on the outside.

The natives wanted what we had, namely cloth for clothes, and we wanted what they had, food. Bananas, coconuts, and condensed milk. Willem, though now only seven years old, had become an expert at spotting tradable articles. His best finds were the discarded mattresses. Carefully ripping the ticking from the top and bottom, he'd stand back as the clouds of bedbugs rose into the air. They didn't bother him in the least. He'd simply shake out the fabric and roll it into a neat bundle. Then he would head straight for the fence and listen for patrolling guards. If he heard nothing, he would gently separate a few slats of the bamboo matting and poke a small strip of fabric through the hole.

This was the signal that someone inside had fabric to trade. It worked like magic each time. Once the connection had been made and the coast was clear, the trading could begin. The natives were desperate for fabric of any size. Most of them lived in extreme poverty and had only loincloths on their bodies and a roof over their heads, which they shared with a large extended family. They slept on dirt floors and ate from a communal pot. They were in such need of fabric that they always managed to find some food item to trade. Depending on the size or condition of the fabric, Willem could expect either a small tin of condensed milk or several bananas. He would always bring his prize home to show our mother first, although he knew full well that she would tell him to eat it up himself. If he had a number of bananas, she would ask him to share with us, but she was worried about him. I had overheard her telling a friend that Willem needed this extra food because he was growing so fast. I couldn't wait to become his age. I wanted the extra food, too. When he shared bananas with us, we would eat them slowly, savoring every bite, then we would scrape the inside of the skin until it was almost transparent, and eat the scrapings, too. Nothing was ever wasted.

All of the women were expected to work. Many were assigned to kitchen duty, which was extremely hard work, as it entailed lifting large vats of water and rice to boil over wood-burning fires. It took at least two women to lift the vats with the aid of bamboo poles carried across their shoulders. They stoked the fires with logs they split themselves. Weak and sick with starvation, the women couldn't survive this work for long.

The kitchens had no walls, only a wooden roof to keep off the rains. During the monsoons, the rainwater often blew in at the sides and flooded the dirt floors, extinguishing the wood fires. The women stood ankle-deep in mud as they stirred the rice. At such times, meals were delayed or simply canceled because the wet wood wouldn't burn. Then the smoke from the wet logs hung low in heavy rolls under the ceiling, enveloping the heads of the cooks as they struggled to coax the logs to burn. The only advantage to working in the kitchens was that you were never as hungry as everyone else.

Other women worked on the streets picking up litter, sweeping, or disposing of items such as the mattresses Willem collected for the fabric. These mattresses were so filled with bedbugs that nobody wanted to touch them. Many women worked at the Japanese headquarters cleaning, serving the officers, or helping with paperwork.

My poor mother had the worst job of all. She had to keep the drains and sewer pipes that ran down both sides of the road flowing. I can't help thinking that she got this job because she quietly refused to bend to the whims and fancies of the guards. She was never rude or hostile, kept herself and her children out of their way, but her manner was less obsequious. She still had the audacity to hold her head high.

Since these sewers were the only place where you could empty your potties or buckets of wastewater, the drainage system was blocked more often than not. The sewer would bubble up and overflow into the streets, creeping over sidewalks and up driveways. This sewage, coupled with the intense heat, produced an unbelievable stench that filled every home, living space, and garden, until you almost choked as you gasped for clean air. Mosquitoes and worms flourished, and you struggled desperately not to slip as you stood barefoot for *tenko* in this filthy river of sludge.

To clear the sewers, a large machine consisting of winches and wheels, handles, and iron cables was placed over the opening to the drains. By some intricate means of pushing and pulling, it usually managed to dislodge whatever was blocking the drains, but occasionally they were so hopelessly blocked that my mother would have to go down into the sewer herself to get things flowing again. She would slide down the cables and stand thigh-high in sludge and fecal matter to grope for the offending potties and buckets that had fallen in as they were being emptied and were now the cause of the blockage.

Then she would climb laboriously back up the cable to crank the heavy handle that set the machine in motion again. A Japanese guard would stand idly by, watching as she struggled with her dirty, slippery hands to prevent the crank from spinning out of control. It was extremely hard and brutal work for my mother, but to us children it was a fascinating thing to watch. Groups of children always surrounded the machine as she worked. It looked so easy and like such fun.

One day, quite by chance, we got to try it by ourselves. The street was empty, not a guard in sight. A group of little boys was already lingering around the machine

Admiring the way the cogs fit into one another, they were also touching the strength of the iron cables. I peered down the dark hole of the sewer that smelled so bad. The boys were braver. Several were climbing up the sides of the machine, while others were fingering the crank that turned the cogs. They were everywhere, swinging from the cables and hanging upside down over the sewer hole. It became a daring contest in climbing skills.

We were so totally absorbed in this forbidden exploration that an earsplitting scream made us jump back in fright.

Nobody moved. A little boy near the cranks, not realizing that another had his finger in one of the cogs, had turned the crank to see what it would do. The cog had turned easily and a finger was severed at the knuckle. We were stunned. Clutching his hand and screaming, the injured child ran home while the rest of us stood rooted to the spot. Within minutes, his mother appeared, running down the road toward us, screaming, 'Find his finger! Find his finger!' As we looked on in horrified silence, she hurled herself to the ground and started scratching in the dry soil. In a frenzy, she crawled around on her hands and knees while we stood and watched.

'Is this it?' one of the children asked as he picked up the finger and laid it on a leaf. The mother snatched it up in both hands and hurried down the street, sobbing as she went. Her little boy, still clutching his hand, tried to catch up with her.

Where she went with that finger, we never knew. Obviously, it was never reattached. We children secretly believed that she kept it in a box in case she found someone after the war who could sew it back on.

Days in the camp were long and monotonous, especially during the monsoons. For about five months each year, usually starting in December, the days turned extremely humid and deprived you of any energy. Just when you felt that you could take no more, and tempers were at the breaking point, the monsoon rains of February came sheeting down. All day long the deluge continued, making rivers out of the parched roads. It poured off the roofs and into the doors and windows. Though less oppressive, the air was still so hot and humid that our bodies were soon covered with a prickly heat rash. This rash was so itchy that the only way to get any relief at all was to scratch until you bled. Unfortunately, once the skin was broken, infections set in, inevitable in our filthy living conditions. Out of desperation, my mother sent us out to play in the rain. Dressed in little shorts or underpants, we dashed around excitedly to find the biggest downspouts or the largest puddles where we could wallow and find some blessed relief from the painful itching.

During the monsoons, food was always a problem. It was never wise to save anything, as bread hidden for even half a day was soon covered in pale green mold. The very walls of our garage oozed with damp and slime to the point that the harmless, tiny *tjit-tjaks,* lizards, that loved to crawl up and down the walls preferred to stay outside in the trees. Tempers flared, and fights broke out among the prisoners as the monsoons dragged on for months.

Our mother felt that this was the perfect time to start teaching Willem to read. She carefully wrote out letters on pieces of paper for him. He struggled with words and sentences but eventually began reading whole stories that our mother had painstakingly written down for him. Sitting nearby on the floor, drawing countless pictures, I listened intently to his progress. I loved these lessons. The moment Willem got up and left his precious stories unattended, I grabbed the papers and slowly paged through them, reciting out loud the words I had memorized, though I couldn't read a single one.

One day, in the first rainy season, Willem came rushing home, carefully cradling a dirty cloth sack in his folded arms. He was flushed with excitement and the exertion of running.

'Look, Mum,' he whispered excitedly as he gently opened the sack. 'They gave me these today. Can you believe it? For that dirty old pillow I found yesterday.'

Proudly he displayed three tiny chicks. As soon as they saw daylight, they started to chirp loudly and hopped out of the sack to look for food.

Willem had intended to rip apart the discarded pillow, but that would have made only a small cloth to barter with, hardly worth even one banana. So he had taken it to the barbwire fence, and after first listening intently for any approaching guards, he ever so carefully opened a hole in the matting and beckoned with his finger. Before long, a dark eye appeared on the other side. Willem stood back and held up the pillow, showing only the cleanest side. Different eyes now appeared at the hole. Then a loud discussion, followed by silence.

Confused, Willem pressed his eye to the hole and looked around. There seemed to be no one about. The pillow must not be good enough, he decided. He looked at it again and wondered whether he should rip it apart after all. Just as he was about to grab the fabric, someone called to him through the hole. Willem approached the fence cautiously. A finger was beckoning for him to look through.

What he saw took him completely by surprise. One of the natives was holding up three small chicks by their tiny legs. They dangled upside down, fluttering crazily.

Willem quickly motioned with his head that he would take them. He could hardly believe his luck. Quickly he pushed more bamboo slats aside to enlarge the hole. Then, one by one, the scrawny little chicks were shoved head-first through the opening. As each one appeared, Willem stuffed it into his pocket, at the same time looking around to make sure no guards were coming. Transactions had to be completed quickly, as punishment for being caught at the fence could mean a day's rations.

Now for the pillow. The only way to get it to the other side was to throw it over the top. Voices were already rising on the other side. Willem was getting desperate, as he knew it did not take long for the Indonesians to start worrying that you were cheating them. He was beginning to think he might have to return the little chicks through the fence when the end of a long rope came flying over the top. Two dark eyes were watching him through the hole.

Willem grabbed the rope and tied it around the pillow. The eyes still watched him intently as someone else started pulling. Although the pillow caught on the wire barbs several times, it did finally make it over the top.

Pushing the loosened bamboo slats hastily back across the hole, Willem darted away from the fence. Carefully transferring the chicks to a small sack lying nearby, he dashed home to show off his prize. In his mind's eye, the chicks were already grown and laying eggs. He smiled at the thought of a soft-boiled egg, and he was still smiling as we gathered around to admire his latest acquisition.

I thought they were the most beautiful creatures I had ever laid eyes on. I just wanted to pick them up and hold them. I didn't notice how scrawny and undernourished they were. Their little eyes were almost glued shut with dirt, and their tail ends had been pecked bare of feathers. They struggled to keep their tiny beaks open for air.

We could sense that somehow our mother wasn't as delighted with these new additions to our family as we were. She just looked at them and never said a word. Ever practical, she sent Willem to find a good-size box in which to keep them. Then she found a small tin for their water and placed it in the box. Willem offered his lump of rice for their food, saying he wasn't hungry anyway. But I knew he was lying.

Then he looked at me. I wasn't as prepared to give up my daily treat for his chicks, because I was hungry and

I desperately looked forward to that extra lump. Then I looked at the chicks in the box and felt guilty.

'Oh, all right. They can have it,' I told him with a touch of bitterness.

My guilt had been appeased, but not the excruciating gnawing in my stomach. As if she could sense the enormous sacrifice we had made, my mother felt great pity for us and offered us both an extra lump of rice. 'To celebrate,' she said, giving us a loving hug.

In spite of the gentle care that Willem lavished on the chicks, they failed to flourish. They stood around listlessly and occasionally tried to chirp. A dreadful, guttural bubbling would emerge from their tiny beaks.

'Snot!' one of our neighbors told us.

Willem and I stared in horror at the chicks. 'Snot?' we asked.

'Yes. Chickens often get so full of snot, they can't breathe anymore, and then they die. It's a chicken's disease.'

We peered in at the chicks. At least they were still alive. We didn't believe they had snot. We couldn't see any.

As the days passed, the chicks ate less and less of the rice we placed in their box. The poor frail things simply stood around with their eyes closed. My mother tried to break it to us gently that the chicks would never grow into egg-laying chickens. We didn't have the right food for them, and they were very sick.

I came home unexpectedly one day from a friend's house and found my mother in the back garden acting very strange. She had a big round stick in her hand, with which she was measuring the distance from a small package wrapped in cloth, lying in the middle of the dirt, to where she was standing. With a look of utter pity on her face, she then turned her head away and closed her eyes. Having done so, she whacked wildly in the direction of the package. Once she had hit it several times, she turned around again and stared in its direction for several minutes without moving. Slowly she walked toward it and gently picked it up. Looking down through her tears at the crumpled package, she whispered softly, 'I'm so sorry, little chicks. Believe me, I'm so sorry,' before laying them back in the box.

As I watched, with tears streaming down my cheeks, I couldn't help but feel guilty. I had been too intrigued by her strange performance to turn away, though I knew what she was doing. Although I never let my mother know I had watched her, I think she knew, because I wouldn't go near the box and stayed away from the funeral.

The sad little chicks were only the first in a line of animals or pets we kept in camp. All were designed to feed us at some point, although not many actually made it into our stomachs. Apart from the snails we collected and kept in a large coop, most of the cats and dogs were stolen before we had a chance to eat them. Only a few of the mangy specimens that wandered haplessly into camp ended up in our own pot.

Another day, Willem once again came racing into the garage with great excitement. This time he had brought home two pigeons – full-grown, healthy, fat birds that he received in exchange for fabric torn from a mattress he had found by the side of the road. He scrounged around and found enough wood scraps and chicken wire to build a cage for them. We hung the cage outside our entrance so we could listen to the comforting, cooing noises they made all day. They provided us with a sense that all was well with the world in spite of the turmoil around us. Since they couldn't fly away because of their clipped wings, we would let them out of the cage to scratch around in the dirt for grit and grubs. We gathered seed heads from various grasses and also shared some of our rice rations with them. They were magnificent birds, and we were proud of them. As far as we were concerned, they were no longer destined for our table. We just couldn't do it. But obviously someone else could. Where hunger is a way of life, any source of food is hard to resist. It didn't really matter that the potential food happened to be a little boy's pets.

When Willem went to feed his birds one morning, he discovered the empty cage. Though my big brother seldom cried, he was so heartbroken that he wept bitter tears of loss and anger. Anger that someone had dared to steal what was his. It was especially hard to imagine someone eating his beloved birds. He had loved those pigeons so much. And now they were gone.

———————

At least a year would pass before we again tried to raise a bird for the table. This time my mother got involved. By that time we had moved with several other families to a tiny house close to the barbwire fence. The usual bamboo matting shielded us from the Indonesians living on the outside, but now a deep storm ditch led under the fence from our side to theirs. We often hung our heads way down into the ditch to get a glimpse of the people on the other side. The ditch was not big enough for us to attempt escape, but it was plenty big enough for a fat goose to inch his way under the fence and along the drain into camp. We began to look forward to his visits, like a friend from the outside world, though we never understood why he came so faithfully every day. It certainly wasn't for the food. There was never any left for him. He allowed us to pet him and to hold him on our bony laps. His cold webbed feet sent shivers of delight up our backs. After his brief visits, he would waddle back to the ditch and make his cumbersome way to the outside.

My mother and her friend Bep also began to take a keen interest in this goose. They noted how he came under the fence and how perfectly tame he was. They saw how he never hissed or squawked or flapped around. A nice quiet goose, they said. That was good. He shouldn't be too much trouble. They started to collect pieces of scrap wood, measuring them up against the width of the ditch. They laughed a lot and spoke in low voices. They wanted to be friends with the goose, too, they told us.

Every day they sat with us and stroked and petted the goose as he waddled around their legs. The goose felt quite at home and never suspected a thing. Occasionally my mother even tried holding on to him 'just to see what he would do if he couldn't get away.' Not a squawk. Not a struggle. 'Perfect!'

'How about if we kept him here with us?' she asked one day. We looked at her with surprise. She held her finger to her lips. This was indeed exciting. While we watched, and the unsuspecting goose grazed on any little blade of grass he could find, my mother and Bep scurried to cover the exit in the ditch. They had just enough wood.

All was well until it was time for the goose to return home. We watched intently as he waddled down to the ditch. Then he stopped, craned his long neck, and looked about. We held our breath. He pushed against the feeble partition and pushed again. Realizing suddenly that he couldn't get out, he waddled back over to where we eagerly awaited him with open arms. He wants to stay, we thought happily. He really likes us.

The next instant took us completely by surprise. Stretching his long fat neck and opening his wings wide, he started to honk and squawk and flap as though we were already wringing his neck. The commotion was petrifying. My mother scooped up the goose as best she could and dashed inside with him. But not for one instant did the goose let up his squawking. Now another noise echoed that of the goose. The natives on the other side of the fence had heard the commotion and knew exactly what it was all about. Rocks, stones, and bamboo spears came flying through the air. Angry voices demanded the immediate return of their goose. The barricade in the ditch came crashing in and angry faces appeared, hanging upside down.

'It's no good,' my mother said, 'there is going to be too much trouble if we don't return it.'

'Shame,' said Bep. 'I was really looking forward to a good meal.'

Willem and I were horrified. Eat that goose? We thought he was going to be our new pet. It was strange, but we felt terribly let down by our mother.

As though he knew what our intentions were, the goose kept up his loud squawking until we pushed him safely back under the fence. We really hated to see him go. The natives nailed a permanent partition into place, and we never saw our beloved goose again.

Not only geese traveled through the underworld for a change of scenery. The part of the ditch through which the goose entered was mostly open. There were, however, long stretches where the ditch became a tunnel running just below the surface of a road or field, serving mostly as a drain for water or the overflow of the sewer system. One such drain ran underground a ways from our camp and emerged in a camp of mostly older prisoners. The drains were made of cement and big enough to allow children or small teenagers to crawl through on their bellies. The temptation to do this was just too much for some of the older children in the camp. Crawling through without too much difficulty, they found, much to their surprise, that life was easier in this neighboring camp. These prisoners were obviously not as difficult or as much of a threat to the Japanese as those in our camp. Even more surprising was the fact that they received more food rations. Fortunately, they were happy to share some of the extra food with these children who looked so starved.

Returning from one of their highly risky trips in the evening, the children were about to exit from the narrow tunnel when they became aware of the approach of heavy boots. With pounding hearts, they slowly, ever so slowly slid their bodies, feet first, back into the tunnel. They had to retreat far enough so that it would be difficult to see them in the dark. Lying end to end like sausages strung together, they tried not to breathe too deeply. The air was foul and rank, and now their bodies blocked most of the air.

Trying not to cough or choke, they had only to look at the black boots stationed in front of the exit to realize that it was 'Don't cough, or die a certain death.' The children were sure that the guard was unaware of their presence in the sewer, but it was strange that he had decided to stand guard in that very spot for so long that evening. It was scary enough to convince them that the trip through the sewer was just not worth it, in spite of the extra food.

————

On many occasions, we tried our hand at growing some extra vegetables. Tomatoes, mostly, as those were the easiest seeds to barter for through the fence. Unfortunately, we were never too successful in growing them. The biggest problem was the lack of water. We needed every drop for ourselves. During the monsoons, when the plants could have all the water they needed, they lacked sunshine and soon grew moldy. We resorted to watering the plants surreptitiously with our own urine and were able to grow fairly decent-size tomatoes, only to lose them to pilfering guards who felt no guilt about helping themselves. The last thing we felt compelled to do was supply extra food to those who already had more than they needed, so our attempts at gardening came to a sorry end.

————

When she was not cleaning out sewers, or cutting people's hair in exchange for an extra morsel of food, my mother was knitting. She never went anywhere without her needles and balls of unbleached cotton yarn that the Japanese supplied. Day in, day out, she knitted the long tube socks they wore in their boots. For every pair of socks she handed in, she would receive a small portion of sugar or tea or half a loaf of bread. Unless we had to spend a whole day in line for *tenko,* when it was absolutely forbidden to do anything but bow, she could knit one pair of socks a day. I often went along with her to stand in line and deliver the socks. She'd still be casting off the last stitches as they handed her the meager recompense and more yarn. I held the packet so she could immediately start on the next pair as we walked home.

Many, many years later, after the war, she would laugh as she remembered all those socks she had knitted.

'If only they could have known all the evil and nasty thoughts I knitted into those socks, they never would have worn them,' she told me.

7

Hard Lessons to Be Learned

Time dragged on. We children had gotten used to life in the camp, but it was harder for our mother. She never forgot the wonderful years in her beautiful home in Bandung. For her, the routines of this concentration camp would never feel normal. We were surviving, rather than living. Overcrowding, filth, and hunger were a way of life. Watching her children grow up taking these conditions for granted only made our mother's daily misery worse.

One thing I never got used to in camp was all the fighting. It terrified me. Anything could trigger a fight. Not only among the children but among the adults as well. The sight of women fighting would twist my stomach into such tight knots that I would almost vomit. If my mother was involved, it became more than I could cope with. Of course, the fights usually centered around food. We were all so hungry that getting even one extra teaspoon of rice was cause for blows.

Living space was another problem. Crammed on top of one another, we had no way to get away from our neighbors. Our family was lucky in our little corner of the garage, because our mother had had the foresight to bring the necessities to ensure some privacy, namely the sheets, tablecloths, and rope. Most people had brought mainly clothes, with no thought to how fast the children would outgrow them. In the houses, mattresses lay side by side, much like wall-to-wall carpeting. People had to walk right across them to leave the room. They couldn't help it, but it caused a lot of friction.

Over the years, we were moved around to different locations. In one little house, we were allotted the central hallway as our living space. It was extremely small, but at least it had a doorway and a window. The big drawback was the fact that two tiny rooms led off this hallway. This meant constant coming and going by the people who occupied those rooms.

A meeting was held among the three families to try

and solve this problem. The Jansens were more than willing to use the window in their room as a door, and they soon had a series of steps rigged up. But the Smitts had no intention of clambering in and out of their window. 'Why should we? We have a perfectly good door we can use,' they said.

The Smitt family consisted of a mother, a young daughter, and a son, who, for all intents and purposes, should have been sent to the men's camp. He was a big boy and 'old enough to start shaving,' or so I had overheard my mother telling the woman next door. He didn't come out of his room much, and when he did, it was usually in the late evening. He always wore a scarf around his head, and told us it was because he had a bad cold. We didn't believe a word of it and thought he looked very funny. My mother was forever trying to block his way when he barged through our room to go out. She was starting to get highly annoyed with him.

It was around this time, after we had been in the camp for about two years, that I became very ill. My head hurt so much from a high fever that I couldn't open my eyes or lift my head from the mattress. I hadn't eaten in days, and the only way I could drink any liquids was by spoon, a few drops at a time. My whole body ached so badly that I couldn't be touched, and I needed total quiet. My mother and a neighbor took turns sitting by my side, applying cool cloths to my forehead as I drifted in and out of consciousness.

On one of those afternoons when my mother was sitting quietly by my side, the Smitts' door flew open with a great flourish. The boy came stomping out, followed by his mother and sister, as he shouted words of abuse at anyone who got in his way. From where she was sitting on the floor, my mother jumped up and tried to grab him. Her patience was finished. Mrs. Jansen, who had heard the commotion, came rushing from her room and tried to help my mother. Several more women came in from outside, and there was a lot of shouting and thumping and slapping going on right next to my bed.

I opened my eyes in bewilderment and saw a large, heaving mass of people. They seemed to sway from left to right, pushing and pulling and twisting and turning. Loud, angry shouts were followed by sharp slaps on bare skin. In my agonizing daze, every sound was magnified. The most horrifying sight was my beloved mother right in the center of all this brawling.

I was almost blind with the pain in my head, and my body felt so weak and shaky I didn't feel I had control of it, but I managed to stagger to my feet and tried to distinguish between the swaying bodies fighting and clawing near me. I could see my mother's back. If only I could get ahold of her and beg her to stop. I didn't want her to get hurt. I reached out my arms and leaned forward just as the clump of bodies moved away from the bed. I felt myself flying through the air and falling into a gray emptiness, down and down. Then total silence.

———

Several days passed before I woke up again. It was dark and quiet in the room, and my mother was sitting by my bed gently stroking my hands. She offered me some water and smiled when I lifted my head to drink. The terrible pain and fever were gone, though not the anguish of seeing people brawl. That would stay with me the rest of my life.

I gradually regained my strength, and life went back to normal. The Smitts didn't cross our room anymore; in fact, they didn't live there any longer. I was told that a Japanese officer had come in during the fighting and had taken the boy away to a camp for men. Mrs. Smitt and her daughter were taken to tighter security and punished for hiding such a grown boy.

I remember this little house where the fighting took place very well because my first best friend, Mieke, lived just a few doors down from us. That house was also the place where I told my first major lie.

Mieke and her mother occupied a tiny little room at the front of their house. It was dark and mysterious and totally airless. Mieke's mother had brought a lot of heavy, woven, almost tapestrylike maroon curtains into camp. Apparently she thought they could come in handy for blankets as well as curtains. One of these large curtains completely covered two of their walls, as well as their one small window. This meant that the only light or fresh air that ever entered the room came in when the door was left open.

On this particular day, Mieke was late coming out to play, so I decided to go see what she was up to. Her mother let me in, but it took me a while to adjust to the darkness in the room. When I finally saw my girlfriend, I could not believe my eyes. She was sitting in regal splendor on top of a pile of mattresses that were covered with another of the heavy curtains. She looked like a beautiful princess. Around her neck hung several strings of wooden beads in soft pastel colors, and in her arms she held a cloth doll. I was speechless.

'It's Mieke's birthday today,' her smiling mother told me proudly.

This was too much for me. I couldn't keep my eyes off those beads.

'Really? That's funny,' I said without hesitation. 'It's my birthday, too!' The lie came so easily. I didn't even have to think about it.

'Well, in that case,' said Mieke's mother, sweeping me up into the air and sitting me next to Mieke on the mattresses, 'I'll have to sing to both of you.'

She sang lustily, waving both arms in the air as though conducting, and when the song ended, she placed a string of those beautiful wooden beads around my neck. Now I, too, felt like a princess, a guilty one perhaps, but nevertheless a happy one. Who would ever find out it was not my birthday? This was truly wonderful. I slipped from the bed and said I had to go home. I wanted to be alone with the necklace. I sauntered slowly back, fingering the precious beads and singing softly to myself. I was amazed at my own good fortune.

My mother saw the necklace immediately. 'Oh, that's pretty, where did you get it?' she asked curiously.

'Mieke's mother gave it to me. She made them for us because we are friends.' This lie, too, slipped out easily, and my mother believed it.

Deep down inside, however, I didn't feel comfortable. I tried to stay out of my mother's way for most of the day, doing nothing in particular, when all of a sudden I heard voices out in the road. I recognized the voice of Mieke's mother. She was talking to mine.

'Congratulations on your daughter's birthday,' she said.

My mother, even from a distance, was obviously bewildered. 'It's not her birthday today. Not until August,' she said.

I could tell that Mieke's mother was surprised, but she seemed to understand what had happened.

'Claartje!' my mother called. 'Claartje, come here a minute.'

Heart pounding, I skipped outside as though nothing was wrong. Both women were watching me.

'What did you do wrong today?' my mother asked me sternly.

'Nothing,' I replied, pretending to think about it.

'Think again,' she said as she lifted the precious necklace over my head. She handed it back to Mieke's mother. 'Thank you for letting her wear it all morning,' she said. Turning to me, she said, 'You'd better go back inside until you can remember what you did wrong, and then come and tell me all about it.'

I stomped angrily back into the house and started to cry. I didn't have to think about it. I knew what I had done, but I did so love that beautiful necklace. Defiantly, I stayed inside for several hours, until my mother urged me to walk with her to my friend's house to apologize. It was a lesson I would never forget.

No matter how hard life became, my mother expected us to remain respectful, polite, and, above all, honest.

8

The Monkey

Most of the Japanese guards seemed to possess a mean streak that would manifest itself from time to time in the most unexpected of ways.

One of the guards kept a small monkey as a pet. We felt he didn't really love the animal but was keeping it only as a means of controlling the prisoners. All the children were frightened of it.

At regular intervals, the monkey would escape and terrorize us all with his mad rampages. He was a very skinny, dirty little monkey, his rib cage sticking out well beyond his waistline. Around his middle he wore a tight leather belt. It looked so tight, we were sure his skin was growing over it. From this belt hung a big metal ring to which a rope was attached, and he was usually tied to a post near the Japanese headquarters.

When we children passed by, the monkey lunged and leaped toward us until he came to an abrupt and painful halt at the end of his rope. He bared his sharp yellow teeth and screeched in frustration. Though we knew from past experience what would happen, we still watched in fascination as he fiddled with the knot in the rope until he managed at last to untie it. Then, with a gleeful swoop, he jumped and usually landed right in the middle of the now screaming crowd of children. We scattered in all directions, falling over one another and crying out in excited terror. The guards just looked on and laughed, encouraging the monkey to more vicious acts. They were not the least bit concerned that their monkey might hurt someone.

Since the monkey was half starved, he always seemed to know exactly where any food was stored or hidden. When he got loose, he would head immediately toward those areas to help himself. After some bad encounters with the monkey, nobody ever tried to stop him. One poor woman, who watched as her meager ration of rice disappeared, made the mistake of grabbing for the bowl from the monkey's paws. She ended up with vicious bites all over both arms and needed stitches. But of course there was no doctor. We all thought she was going to die when she became delirious from a high fever.

Whenever the monkey was free, most people tried to stay inside their rooms if at all possible. Sometimes this could last for days. I was often left alone to watch over Gijs, as our mother still had to clear the sewers, and Willem continued to scavenge for fabric to trade. When Gijs was asleep on the mattress, I curled up right next to him, as close as I could without waking him up, because I was frightened that his crying might attract the monkey. When Gijs was awake, I did anything in my power to keep him amused and quiet. I was particularly anxious since we didn't have a proper door to our corner of the garage, only a large hole in the wall. I always made sure that the blanket was well pulled across this opening so that the monkey couldn't see us.

One time, the monkey sat for a whole day on the roof of the house facing our room. Every time I peeked around the blanket, there he was, staring at me. Some of the other prisoners in the house threw stones at him to make him go away, but one of the guards saw them and took them immediately to the commandant. He was extremely angry that people could be so cruel to animals and forced them to give the 'poor monkey' their ration of food for the day. After that, nobody dared do anything to the monkey, even when he grabbed our precious food rations. We just tried to hide the food better.

Though he scared us children more than he hurt us, the monkey seemed to genuinely dislike women. One day a mother was running after her toddler, not realizing that the monkey was anywhere in the area, when he swooped down from a tree and bit her very hard on the head. He wouldn't let go until one of the guards pulled him off. As if this wasn't bad enough, the woman was then severely punished for running. Didn't she know she was scaring the poor monkey?

———

By the time we had been living in camp for two years, we were weak, tired, and always hungry. Our heads were teeming with lice, our bodies covered with prickly heat rashes, and we had all come down with amoebic dysentery. We all had bloody diarrhea. Unfortunately, the potty had to stand near the door, since the stench in our small living space would have been unbearable if we had put it in a more private spot.

It was during one of the monkey's rampages that I was

forced by the terrible pains in my stomach to get up in the middle of the night to use the potty. The blanket that usually covered the doorway was pulled to one side to let in the cool night air. It was dark and extremely quiet outside when all of a sudden, just to the right of where I was sitting and immediately outside our doorway, there was a scuffling noise.

My heart froze in terror. I could hardly breathe and started to choke as fear constricted my throat. The painful gurglings inside my stomach seemed awfully loud all of a sudden. I was well aware of the consequences of being up and about after curfew, let alone making any noise. I sat as still as I could and strained my eyes to see. To my utter horror, a long, dark arm reached over my head into the room and deposited something onto our chest of drawers beside me.

I had seen enough. In one bound, I landed on the mattress next to my mother, screaming in terror. I was convinced that the monkey had grown into a full-size gorilla and had come to get me. Could it be the same one that lived in the ceiling in Bandung? My mother sat bolt upright in bed and grabbed me just as another body hurled itself onto the mattress beside us. But it was already too late. Heavy footsteps came running down the path and stopped outside our little room.

The squat figure of a guard darkened our doorway.

'What's going on in here?' he screamed angrily.

'Nothing. My little girl is having a nightmare,' my mother answered. 'She'll be all right now. I'm sorry. Good night.'

All this time she was burying my face into her neck to stop my screaming. The guard tried to peer into the room, but it was too dark for him. He got up slowly and walked away, shouting and giving a few vicious whacks with his club to the garage wall. We didn't move, just simply sat hugging each other until we stopped shaking. Behind me, the body that had hurtled onto the mattress stirred.

'Oh my God, that was close,' someone whispered with a big sigh. 'But now what am I going to do?'

It was Johanna, a woman who had entered the camp the same day as us but had no intention of staying any longer. She was young and alone, and was planning an escape with several other prisoners. She had come to return something belonging to my mother before joining the others at the barbwire fence. Unfortunately, my terrified outburst had ruined their chance of a successful escape. Even my mother would now be implicated, as there had been a disturbance in the night inside our little room. The guards were suspicious of anything out of the ordinary and would be extra watchful for a while.

We sat without moving, almost not daring to breathe, in case the guard was still around. It would be dangerous for all of us if he returned and found Johanna in our room. Prisoners were not supposed to move around at night. After straining to hear any little noises that might give away the guard's proximity, my mother crept over to the doorway. Reluctantly she stuck her head out to double-check that all was clear and then, under her breath, called Johanna to her side. I could hear my mother begging her not to try her escape now.

'I have three small children,' she pleaded softly. 'I can't risk anything. Please, for their sakes, don't try anything tonight.'

For a brief moment they stood without speaking, both thinking about the consequences of a rash decision. My mother didn't feel it was necessary to plead further.

'All's quiet,' she whispered. 'Good luck.'

Johanna slipped out into the night and was gone.

My mother sat down just inside our room and looked up at the sky. She sat for a long time, and I knew she was praying.

The next day at *tenko* we saw Johanna in her line. Her

face was swollen from crying, but she smiled at my mother. My mother smiled back and I heard her whisper to herself, 'Oh, thank you, God.'

9

The Winner?

Like all seven-year-old boys, Willem liked to be considered strong and brave. He would hang from tree limbs, jump over high stumps, or lift anything that seemed at all heavy, just to prove his own strength. He would never cry when he was hurt or frightened, and even allowed his loose tooth to be pulled out with a string. His favorite expression, especially to me, was always 'I bet you can't do this.' More often than not I couldn't, and I didn't really care to, either. On this particular day, however, I felt I had to prove him wrong.

We were standing in front of a pile of rocks, all shapes and sizes. The idea was to see who could lift the biggest one. We would start with the smallest and work our way up. Simple! His rocks always seemed slightly larger than mine, however, and he would look at me disdainfully as I stuck to the smaller ones.

'Girls,' he whispered mockingly.

All right, I thought, as I picked up the biggest and most jagged rock on the pile. It was more than I had bargained for. I could feel my face growing red from exertion while my fingers ached from the sharp edges. Willem looked at me in amazement. Desperately, I held on to the rock as the perspiration trickled down my cheeks.

'I bet I can find a bigger one than that,' he said, searching the rock pile. Still I held on to the rock. Not because I didn't want to put it down but because I couldn't. The rock was simply too heavy to throw away from myself. I knew that if I dropped it, it would land on my toes. Willem looked back at me.

'Put it down,' he commanded.

My fingers ached, and I could feel the rock slipping. With a dull thud, it landed right where I thought it would.

I didn't cry or scream or jump up and down. I couldn't say a word. The pain was too excruciating. I thought I was going to vomit. I simply had to walk away.

'Wait! It's my turn now,' Willem yelled.

I couldn't explain. The pain was churning up my insides.

'You didn't win yet, because it's not the end of the game,' he shouted after me. But I was too embarrassed to explain.

By midafternoon the pain had become unbearable. I could no longer be brave. 'I think I hurt my toe, Mummy.'

Willem looked grumpily in my direction as my mother bent down to look at my foot.

'Oh, my heavens!' she exclaimed as she took one look at the swollen and weeping toe. All around the nail the skin was oozing, and the toe resembled a squashed tomato. It does not take long in the tropics for even a small cut to turn into a major festering sore, especially under the conditions in which we were living.

'Come,' she said as she picked me up. 'We'll have to go see the nurse. Let's hope she will have something to make you all better.'

I'd never seen her look so worried before as she ran down the street, holding me in her arms, and up the narrow, dirty staircase to the room where the nurse lived. Her mattress was in the far corner of a large room that she shared with many other women. In her anxiety to reach the nurse, my mother almost tripped over several women asleep on their mattresses.

'Nurse, could you please take a look at my daughter's toe? She has hurt it so badly. It doesn't look good.' She sounded desperate.

The kindly old nurse motioned my mother to lay me down on the mattress. A prisoner like us, she was the only woman with any medical background. Everyone flocked to her for help, knowing they would never be turned away. She had entered camp with her suitcases filled with medical supplies, but they were fast disappearing. If the guards had had any inkling at all of her activities, her supplies would have been confiscated long ago, and she would have been severely punished. As it was, she had to sew many of her bandages, aspirins, surgical instruments, and medications into different areas of her mattress. She was always worried that they would be discovered when the guards went on their camp searches. Luckily for her, the guards usually kicked everyone's belongings around with their heavy boots and never felt the lumpy parts in the mattress.

After taking a quick look at my toe, she told my mother to follow her through a door onto a small balcony at the back of the house. This is where she liked to see her patients. It was hidden from the road and sheltered by trees.

On the balcony she had set up a small table and a

chair. She indicated to my mother to lay me across the table while she checked her bag to make sure she had everything she would need. My mother held my hands as she and the nurse leaned over my foot and examined my throbbing toe. I saw the glances passing between them but couldn't hear what they said. The table was hard on my skinny back as I stared up into the branches of the tree, and I was feeling very nervous. I wished I hadn't played that silly game. My mother suddenly bent over me and put one arm over my chest and her other arm across both my knees. She looked at me and smiled.

'This will hurt a bit, darling,' she said, 'but I know you are such a brave girl.'

I wasn't feeling a bit brave. I couldn't see what the nurse was doing, but I knew she had taken things out of her case. Everything seemed so terribly serious all of a sudden that I became extremely frightened. Tears welled up in my eyes, and I could no longer see my mother through them. She bent down to kiss me just as a hot, searing pain shot through my foot, and a sharp tug made me grab hold of the sides of the table. I sat bolt upright in spite of my mother's arms trying to keep me down, and looked around in confusion.

'There we are. All done.' The nurse was searching for

some clean wrappings. 'We just pulled out your big toenail so your poor toe can get all better.'

This horrible piece of news, accompanied by the most excruciating pain, finally broke me down. I sobbed shamelessly in my mother's arms. Thanking the nurse profusely and promising her a free haircut in payment, my mother carefully carried me back home, where the more difficult task of keeping the wound clean would be her responsibility. Unfortunately for me, there were no painkillers to get me through the next few days.

Willem was sitting on the stoop in front of our entranceway, a look of utter misery on his face. The sight of my mother carrying me in her arms, and the story of the nail-pulling, seemed to add to his dejection. He came and stood beside me as I lay on the mattress with my foot raised. For the longest time, he never said a word, just stared from my foot to my face and back to my foot. Then, so quietly I almost didn't hear him, he whispered, 'I think you won.'

10

Kite Battles

It was up to us children to amuse ourselves every day. A lot of mothers tried to keep up with their children's education by forming study groups for different age levels. They thought it would feel more like school if the children studied this way. This worked for a while, but there were too many instances when children were unable to attend due to sickness, long *tenkos,* or simply lack of energy. Mothers soon got frustrated at the children's inability to concentrate because of hunger. Though the groups disbanded fairly quickly, some mothers continued to teach their own children.

All mothers had jobs to attend to, so there were

many hours when we were left to our own devices. There were few toys around, as they had not ranked as important items when we had to decide what to bring with us into camp. During the monsoon season, this was not a problem. The many flooded ditches provided hours of fun. Sailing sticks, bits of bark, or leaves kept us absorbed for hours. Running along beside the fast-flowing water to keep up with our sailing crafts, we would scream and yell with excitement. Battles would inevitably develop as we argued over who had won. Mud was another marvel to keep us occupied. We spent hours digging and building and creating wondrous forts for imaginary soldiers. Usually it was the girls against the boys.

The dry season was a different matter. If you were lucky enough to get ahold of a coconut, you could cut it in half and hollow it out. Threading a long string through the center, you turned it into a pair of 'horse-shoes.' By standing on the round ends with the string between your toes and holding tightly on to the string, you could clop down the streets and pretend you were riding Black Beauty. Those of us who had tins instead of coconuts were considered owners of thoroughbreds.

For a long time, the most popular activity in camp for children was making kites. It took endless patience and skill to produce the perfect kite. The thin bamboo crosspieces were cut from the groves all around camp, but the light, almost transparent paper and the balls of string had to be bartered from the natives through the barbwire. Willem made the glue himself.

A type of pine tree that grew in several places around camp could be tapped for the sticky substance by making a big gash in the trunk. We collected this sticky substance into a small tin and boiled it over a wood fire until it turned into a thick, dark glue. It was perfect for making kites.

It was our mother who taught Willem how to carefully attach the slender bamboo strips with string to form the frame. Then, laying the frame on the paper, she showed him how to cut just enough paper to fold over the edges and glue into place. He learned quickly, and when he had enough paper and string, Willem made up several kites and spent all day flying them one by one.

They were his passion, and his kites became bigger and better with time. We watched them soaring high above the camp like free spirits, sometimes crossing over the barbwire fences and into freedom. Willem would lie on his back holding the string, enjoying the tug and pull as the kite tried to escape into the deep blue sky. It was a wonderful way to spend a hot afternoon – until something unexpected happened one day.

From the other side of the fence a new kite rose up, with a single red eye painted on its underside. It stared menacingly down at us, as though daring us to come closer. Willem's kite was flying high at this time, its iridescent tail zigzagging lazily in the hot sun. We were lying on our backs and couldn't help but stare at this new phenomenon. Somehow it made us feel ill at ease. There was something so ferocious about the way it darted back and forth. Higher and higher it went, and all the while that evil eye stared down at us. Willem started reeling in his kite, though it seemed reluctant to come down. All of a sudden, without warning, the evil eye dove across his kite string with its own, and in no time had severed his string in two. Willem's precious kite spiraled down from the sky and fell into enemy territory.

'Hey!' he shouted, jumping up and rushing over to the fence. But he knew it was useless. A cheer had already gone up from the other side as his kite landed. We watched in disbelief and anger as the eye was reeled in and disappeared behind the fence, too.

Willem was heartbroken. That was his favorite kite. It flew so beautifully, and it was the only one with a colored tail. We walked home dejectedly, winding what was left of the string back onto the stick. Luckily, he still had his other kites hanging on the wall.

It was several days before there was enough wind to fly a kite again. Willem and a couple of his friends decided to hold some races, just to see who could get his kite up the fastest and highest. A few practice runs were allowed, to adjust tails and to rearrange strings on the bamboo ribs, and then the kites were off.

Up and up they soared, dipping and diving, shuddering and free-falling, to be jerked back by only a quick tug on the string. Four kites soared into the great blue sky, weaving from side to side like a slow waltz with the wind. It was a beautiful sight, and all our heads were thrown back, absorbed in keeping the strings untangled, when, out of nowhere, darted the Evil Eye once more.

It rose so fast from the other side of the fence that no one had time to reel in his own kite. Its red eye staring menacingly down from its belly, it crossed all four strings, touched each one briefly, and then took off into the sky above their village. The four kites fluttered down like wounded birds and landed on the other side of the fence. The taunting cheer rose again. We were dumbfounded. How could that happen? How could one string be cut so easily by another?

Though the winds would have been perfect for flying, several days passed without the kites going up. Willem was searching for a clue as to what made the Evil Eye so powerful. He didn't want to lose any more kites, as he had run out of paper and string.

It became obvious that the natives on the other side were anxious to continue their quest for kites. To taunt us into battle, they flew Willem's favorite kite, the one with the colored tail, over the fence and just out of reach. On its underside they had painted a large grinning mouth. We stared at it in disbelief. If only we could reach up and pull it down. The wind brought the kite farther and farther over the camp.

The other boys had seen it, too, and came running to Willem's side. They soon decided to raise one of their own kites and to entangle the strings with the enemy in order to bring it down. This was their only chance, but they had to act fast. The wind was in the right direction, and their kite shot up into the sky. It headed straight for the grinning mouth as Willem let out his string. It almost flopped out of control when the string unreeled too fast. At the same instant, the natives had become aware of the kite and had pulled tight on their own string. This had brought the grinning mouth up and under Willem's kite, trapping it. Perfect. He grabbed the string and tugged until the two kites came tumbling from the sky. The grinning mouth lay in a tattered heap in the dirt on our side of the fence. The natives were still trying to pull on the string, but it was already caught on the barb-wire and would not budge further. This time it was our turn to let out a loud cheer.

More than just revenge, this episode provided the clues Willem had been looking for. He discovered that the string, which had so mercilessly cut his, was glass string. Tiny particles of glass — glass dust, as it were — were somehow glued onto the string. When the glass string rubbed against regular string, it cut the other in half. This knowledge somehow made up for the degradation of seeing his own favorite kite smiling down at him from the sky. He tore the stupid grin from the kite.

That evening, Willem busied himself with boiling several tins of glue and soaking yards and yards of kite string in it. While it soaked, he gathered all the glass shards he could find, and he and his friends pounded and scraped and crushed the glass into fine powder. It took several days of powder-making before they had enough to sprinkle carefully over the glue-soaked string. The sticky glass string was then carefully suspended from tree branches to dry. By the time Willem had finished this job, his fingers were sore and bleeding.

While the string was drying, Willem and his friends busied themselves with making several more kites. They felt confident that this time they would beat the natives at their own game.

The natives continued to fly their kites low over the fence, taunting us into battle. But Willem and his friends were not ready yet. They were waiting for the perfect time. Willem realized that the glass string had to be completely dry to cut another string in two. The kites also had to be a little larger this time, as glass string was quite a bit heavier than regular string.

The natives on the other side were becoming anxious. In their high-pitched voices, they were screaming abusive language through the fencing. It was definitely time.

'Don't get into trouble,' our mother warned as she lingered to watch the kites for a while; if only she could stay. But someone had told her that a sewer farther down was blocked and nearly overflowing into the road. Better do the job immediately, as she did not want a Japanese officer coming to her room for any reason. The job repulsed her no end, and she knew she would not be able to cleanse herself of the horrible smell that would linger on her body for days after. She moved on reluctantly, her head bent low. She felt so weak and tired.

'How much longer, dear Lord? How much longer?' she would remark.

The kites were already going up. Slowly at first, then catching the wind, they shuddered and twisted and soared into the air. Would they be too heavy? We all held our breath. They looked so magnificent. We were beginning to hope there wouldn't be a battle after all. It would be such a shame to spoil these beauties.

What happened next took us all by surprise. From the other side of the fence rose not three or four but at least a dozen kites. Like a rolling wave of color they advanced toward our meager few. Derisive, mocking laughter accompanied their advance, and Willem and his friends tried to reel in their strings, though they knew that it was already too late. With thumping heart, Willem shouted to his friends to ease the strings, allowing the kites to soar up and beyond the enemy line. Their strings were crossed with the others' before the enemy even realized what was happening or could see that all Willem's strings were glass strings like theirs.

'Now cut!' Willem screamed as he sawed with his string.

Half a dozen of the enemy kites came fluttering down like confetti at a party. Though this was exactly what the boys had been hoping for, they couldn't really believe that their strategy had worked. Carrying the fallen kites like trophies over their heads, they walked about for days with big grins on their faces and the feeling that they could now conquer the world.

Sad to say, their triumph took away some of the joy of simply flying kites. They looked for more competition with the natives now that they knew they stood an equal chance of winning, but the natives were sore losers and could never be persuaded to fly their kites again. Even after all the heartache and hard work, the boys could barely accept the fact that the kite battles were over. Just flying a kite for its sheer beauty and grace, as it dipped and soared above, seemed tame by comparison. But, for a short while at least, the excitement had helped time to pass more quickly in an otherwise dreary march of days.

11

Long, Hot Days

Life for my mother was becoming more and more of a
struggle. The beriberi she had been suffering from for
well over one year was definitely getting worse. The
disease, brought on by malnutrition, caused her legs to
swell up like water-filled bags and made walking difficult and painful. Her movements were slow, but she
never complained. Gijs was an active toddler by now and
often took off on his own, knowing my mother could
not keep up with him when he ran. She pinned pieces
of paper with his name and address onto his clothes.
Sometimes she tethered him to a long rope so she could
keep him in sight.

The hardest times of the day for her were the *tenkos,* the endless standing and bowing in the broiling sun. With perspiration rolling down her face, she would struggle to hold Gijs in her arms while trying to keep her place in line. Little children were to be controlled, or the mothers would be punished. The orders were very strict.

It was noon, the hottest time of the day. A white haze shimmered over the camp, and absolutely nothing stirred. We had eaten our meager meal and were stretched out on the mattress for a nap when the dreaded sirens started wailing. What could possibly be the matter? It had to be something serious, as we knew very well that the guards would never come out during the heat of the day if they could avoid it. Having just fallen asleep, Gijs was not happy to be so noisily awoken. He tried to compete with the earsplitting sirens by howling.

Two and a half years old now, he slept between us on the mattress, as he had long outgrown his wooden drawer. Lifting his angry little body, my mother tried to calm him down as she urged Willem and me to hurry and join her in line. The guards were impatient and expected immediate response when they called.

The heat outside was stifling as disgruntled prisoners tried to form into lines on the melting asphalt in the street. Since so few of us possessed shoes, it was hard to stand still, and blisters formed on the soles of our feet. Willem and I stood one behind the other, while our mother stood directly to our right.

She was struggling to hold on to the wriggling Gijs, who desperately wanted down. His curly blond hair was matted with perspiration and his little cheeks bright red with anger. The more he struggled, the more slippery he became. My mother's perspiring arms on his naked little body made it almost impossible to keep hold of him, but nobody would help her for fear of punishment. The commandant was already on his way, and who knew what could be the reason for this unexpected inspection?

If only the sirens would stop their shrill summons! Our nerves were almost at breaking point.

'*Keirei!*' The order to bow down rang out loud and clear. And still Gijs screamed. His voice could be heard above everything else. He had worked himself into such a frenzy that he couldn't stop. My mother was starting to droop with the heat and fatigue. As she bowed down, she let go all of a sudden and stood Gijs on the ground. The result was immediate. He stopped crying and stood absolutely still. The overwhelming relief was felt by everyone in line.

'*Naore!*' The order to straighten up was given.

'*Keirei! Naore!*' Down! Up! Down! Up! We kept on

bowing as the sun beat down and the commandant made his slow, important way up the lines. As he neared, we were expected to hold our bodies in the bowed position with our eyes on the road. The Japanese officers did not like to be looked straight in the eyes. It was demeaning. We were dirt.

It was at this point, when the commandant and his entourage were several lines down the road, that Gijs decided to go exploring. He slipped through my mother's hands and made his way between the lines. We were all bowing at this time, but rather than let him get too far away, my mother left her line, still in the bowed position, and scurried after him to the front. She managed to grab him just before he reached the open street. As quickly as she could, she walked backward to her place beside us, dragging Gijs by his arm. I smiled at her, but she was still bowing and did not see me. Nobody dared to look at her.

'*Naore!*' The command to straighten sent a cold chill down our spines. It was so close, so loud, and so very angry. The heavy boots had slapped their way between our lines to stop in front of my mother. I think our very hearts had stopped beating at that moment.

My mother stood very still, holding on to Gijs. Then she did the unthinkable. She looked the officer straight in the eyes. Not angrily. Not degradingly, and certainly not in a pleading manner. Simply as a mother who had no choice but to go after her recalcitrant child.

The siren had miraculously stopped wailing. All of a sudden it was silent, as if the very world stood still, and everyone had stopped breathing. Not a movement, not a sound but the thumping of my heart.

I wanted to rush to my mother's side and cry out, 'Don't take my mother away, please! Don't take her away!' But my feet wouldn't move, and my throat was too parched to utter a single sound. I thought my body had turned to stone. The white sun beat down unmercifully, but I did not feel its heat. I stared at my mother's face and could see nothing else.

The officer stood in front of her for several minutes, as though he were deciding what to do. Obviously this woman should be punished, severely punished, for breaking the Imperial Japanese Army's rules. We were all prepared for the worst.

To our amazement, after what seemed like an eternity, he turned sharply, clicked his heels, and stomped back up the line just in time to shout *'Keirei!'* as the commandant reached our section. We bowed in grateful and stunned silence. Looking over at my mother, I suddenly realized that she was crying, that her whole body was shaking, and I sadly turned my eyes away. I knew she would not have wanted me to see her like that, and my eyes started to fill with tears.

We never found out why we were called out in the ungodly heat that day.

———————

We were lucky that time. Not all transgressions were so easily forgiven. Several days later, the sirens summoned us all into the streets again. It was early and still relatively cool, and we were well rested. We didn't expect to be there long, so our spirits were high. The guards sauntered back and forth at the front of the lines, a non-threatening presence, a mere reminder not to become unruly. But the hours dragged on. The heat intensified, and the guards grew impatient. They would no longer tolerate the whispering that had been going on or our sitting down to ease tired and cramping legs. Anybody caught sitting could expect a hearty kick with a heavy boot, or a sharp poke with the butt of a rifle. We tried hard to avoid any such violence to our emaciated bodies, as it brought hours of agonizing pain.

The morning's good feeling was long gone. Fatigue had set in with the heat, and people were starting to faint from lack of water and food. Gijs had fallen asleep in my mother's arms. I could tell she was having a hard time holding him up as her body swayed heavily from side to side on her swollen legs, but she simply stared ahead and held on.

My attention wandered from her to focus on two women standing in the line immediately to my left. I didn't know where they came from, but that didn't really surprise me. People were moved around constantly, from one camp to another or from one house to another. It depended on available space. These days, the barbwire around camp was being pulled in, in ever-tightening circles. Houses that were once inside the fence now stood empty on the outside. The hundreds of prisoners who had once occupied those houses were crammed into the remaining and already overflowing homes. Angry women and children fought daily over their rights for living spaces, and stress and frustration escalated into fistfights as they begged for privacy and just a little quiet.

'Don't step over me,' they cried. 'Can't you go another way?'

'Do you have to go out so many times?'

'Can't you settle down?' Irritated voices argued day and night as people tried to get some rest. Overcrowding had become a major problem. Stress, disease, and smaller portions of food were finally taking their toll. The commandant's careful plan was beginning to work. He was determined to see an end to these hateful women.

If people died, their empty mattresses were quickly allocated to others. That is probably how these two new women came to be in the line next to ours.

I thought they were the most beautiful women in the world. They were tall and slender, with chestnut-brown hair that fell to their shoulders in cascading curls and waves. They wore dresses of brightest red and palest pink, full skirts gathered tightly at the waist with a belt, and best of all, the highest-heeled shoes I had ever seen. To top it all, they both had on bright red lipstick. I couldn't keep my eyes off them. I wanted to wear pretty dresses and high-heeled shoes someday. My handmade shorts, cut from the sheets and tablecloths we had brought with us, suddenly looked very dowdy. These women must have just arrived at camp, with suitcases full of pretty clothes, I thought. Nobody in camp still had decent clothes to wear. In my eyes, these ladies had to be princesses. Oh, to be like them!

The two women seemed totally unaffected by the heat. They were turned toward each other, deep in conversation. They were having a wonderful time, laughing and joking and gesticulating with their arms,

totally oblivious to the world around them. I was fascinated. How on earth did they balance on those heels?
For a moment I did not feel the heat, either. I was living
in a world with princesses, where you did not feel hunger
or thirst or fear. Where you felt fresh and cool in a pretty
dress. Where you danced on high-heeled shoes and felt
happy. I was one of them now, twirling in rainbow circles,
faster and faster and faster until our skirts swung straight
out and—

Thwack! Thump! Smack! My dream quickly disappeared
and my princesses crumpled to the ground with heavy
thuds. Startled into letting out a scream, I hugged my
arms tightly across my stomach.

I had been so wrapped up in my own beautiful world
that I had become oblivious to my surroundings. The
officer had appeared out of nowhere. With one swift
lunge, he swung the butt of his rifle across the women's
heads and sent them reeling to the ground. Then the
heavy boots trampled and stomped and kicked until the
beautiful bodies looked like limp, bloody rags.

And still the boots kept on kicking. First the stomach
and the ribs, and then, for good measure, their faces. The
bright red lipstick was now a smeary mess mixed with
the blood that ran into their hair and dribbled down
their necks.

The bodies lay lifeless at our feet. I heard my mother urgently whispering my name, but I could not tear my eyes away from my princesses. 'Get up! Oh! Please get up!' I whispered, trying to will them back to life. My legs were trembling violently and my stomach was cramping so badly that I felt my very insides were being torn out of me. Still I could not look away. This should not happen to princesses.

'You will obey!' The officer who had done all the kicking was screaming at us all. He was marching back and forth, white with anger and waving his arms in all directions.

'You are rude! You are lazy! You are dirty! You *will* be punished!' he screamed. 'You are dishonorable women who will be taught respect! *Keirei!*'

We stayed in the bowed position while he continued to scream obscenities and abuse and stalked up and down the lines between us. People, mostly the older ones who could not keep the bowed position for that long, fell to the ground and lay there. Others, who had lost control of their bladders from fear, were slapped and beaten until they lay on the ground in their own puddles.

The day that had started with so much promise turned out to be one of the longest and cruelest. We were kept out in the stifling heat until the sun went down. Without water or food all day, many of the prisoners collapsed. My beautiful princesses never got up again. Through my tears, I looked at their lifeless bodies, and every time I bowed down, I had ample opportunity to study the big black flies that settled on the dried blood and swarmed over their poor battered faces.

A cold numbness came over my body, and my legs stopped shaking. I had accepted one more fact of life here – that these two beautiful women would never again dress in pretty clothes, or laugh and smile, because they had broken the harsh rules of the Imperial Japanese Army with their carefree spirit.

They were picked up by the cleanup crew after we had all returned to our quarters, and taken to the front gates where they would eventually be buried in a mass grave.

In grim silence, we stumbled back to our little room in the garage. Her face ashen and her arms around our shoulders to comfort us, our poor mother struggled to walk. Her legs were so puffed up from standing all day that they dimpled when you touched them with a fingertip. She couldn't wait to get inside and lie down to ease the pain. Carefully she stepped over the threshold into our room, then uttered a cry of dismay.

We crowded in beside her and looked around. The room

had been turned upside down and inside out. Every plate, cup, bowl, or glass lay in shards on the floor. Every drawer, suitcase, and box had its contents emptied and strewn around the room. The few precious rations we were saving, in case of more missed meals, lay trampled in the dirt and were now totally inedible. Why had they done this to us again? What were they looking for this time?

With tears streaming from his eyes, Willem crawled frantically amid the fragments on the floor, searching desperately for any morsels of food that could be saved.

'Oh no! Oh please – I'm so *hungry!*' he wailed. Our mother quickly sat beside him on the floor and held him in her arms. She kissed the top of his head and her tears fell into his hair.

'I'll never forgive them,' she murmured angrily.

No wonder we were kept outside all day. These kinds of raids meant only one thing: The Japanese were again suspicious that radios or newspapers had been smuggled into camp through the barbwire fences. We were not allowed to know what was happening in the outside world. Up to this point they had been most successful, as we had no idea how the war was progressing.

Slowly and listlessly, we started to pick up the pieces. There was no way to salvage the food. The guards had made sure of that. Scraping it together, we threw it out with the broken dishes. This was very hard to do, as we knew for certain that we would not get any food today. Willem dejectedly went out to fetch a bucket of water for drinking and bathing, and then it was time for bed. Gratefully, we sank down onto the mattress, too tired to worry about anything else. Our mother reached for the Children's Bible and slowly paged through it until she came to one of our favorite stories. We never tired of hearing how Jesus wouldn't let us starve to death as long as we believed in him. Just look at all the people he fed with just two fishes and five loaves of bread.

As she was reading, she suddenly remembered our precious cod-liver oil. Running her hands quickly along the sides of the mattress where she had hidden the little bottles, our mother discovered to her utmost relief that they were still intact. The mattress had been overlooked as a hiding place.

How wonderful that cod-liver oil tasted. Our mother carefully doled out two small teaspoons each, instead of just one. She never took any for herself.

Staring upward from where I lay, I blinked in surprise. 'Oh look!' I whispered happily, glad to point out that not everything was bad today. 'They didn't touch *that*.' Our mother's beloved painting of the flamboya tree was hanging on the wall, miraculously untouched by the guards. This meant that, for now, our little home remained intact, and we fell asleep knowing that tomorrow was another day, praying that it would be a better one.

12

Three Brave Women

Unfortunately, things got worse before they got better. It was 1944, and the war was dragging on longer than anyone had expected. We had now been in the camp for over two years.

Sickness. Beatings. Deaths. Survival. To us children it had become our way of life. It was all that we knew. We were so young when we entered camp that we could barely remember the days when we didn't feel hungry, thirsty, or frightened. The days that weren't ruled by sirens, heavy boots kicking, or words screamed at us with hatred.

They told us we were filthy vermin, and we were

starting to believe them. It was perfectly true that we were dirty. We had little water and no soap. Sand was all right to scrub our plates clean, but it did not do much for our bodies, covered in open sores. There was little need to wash our plates, anyway, as we usually licked them spotlessly clean – carefully around the edges, since the tins now serving as our plates were sharp where they had been cut. We were receiving only rice now, one very small bowl per day. We did not deserve more food than that, we were told, because we were lazy and ungrateful.

———

Because of the deteriorating conditions in camp – terrible overcrowding, less food and water, and more filth and disease – three brave women took it upon themselves to try to improve life for everyone. They thought they would start by complaining about the quantity and quality of the food, since everyone was starving, and hundreds were dying every day.

They knew they would have to go straight to the commandant, but they also knew they would have to wait for the right moment to approach him. He suffered from manic depression and could fly into uncontrollable rages and bizarre behavior, especially during times of the full moon. Stories abounded that he had been seen balancing precariously in the topmost branches of a tree, trying to scratch the moon out of the sky. 'Hope to God he falls out and breaks his bloody back' was the bitter comment that usually accompanied those stories.

He was also a heavy drinker who turned meaner and more ruthless with every drop of alcohol he consumed. He would then seek relief from his own misery by torturing the prisoners. He loved to use his fists and would go in search of those he felt might give him trouble sometime in the future.

These days he was not at all happy about the state of his camp. In his eyes, the women and children were not dying fast enough. Obviously, the mothers were looking after the children too well. He would have to separate them, but for now he would start by reducing the food portions still further. A few more drinks would help him carry out the threat. It always amused him to see women and children staring blankly into the sky, expecting to see food parcels parachuting down out of nowhere. He'd laugh derisively with his friends, saying, 'They'll believe anything.'

Hunger had become such a problem that people were hallucinating about food parcels arriving in all sorts of miraculous ways. They swore that they had seen the parcels swinging down from the skies but hadn't been able to find them because the guards got to them first. Many times Willem and I eagerly joined crowds at the entrance gates, waiting for the arrival of the American and British soldiers who were going to come sweeping into camp on roller skates, carrying huge bags of food on their backs. Or so we'd heard.

'But, Mum, we'll get left out,' we cried in frustration when our mother tried to hold us back. 'Wouldn't you like some extra food? How do you *know* they're not coming?'

We were desperate to believe in the arrival of any food at all.

––––––––

For days the three women took turns watching for the commandant's arrival into camp. Now that they had made up their minds to talk to him, they were anxious to get it done before they lost their courage.

Finally the day came. The commandant descended from his chauffeur-driven car, waving and smiling at the camp children playing in the street, and patting a small boy on the head as he went into the Japanese head-quarters. This was a good sign.

After cleaning up as best they could and putting on their least ragged shorts and blouses, the three of them walked resolutely into the headquarters and asked to speak to him.

They were shown into a small, dark office where the commandant was seated behind a metal desk, helping himself to the chocolate from the American Red Cross parcels meant for the prisoners. In spite of being caught red-handed, he continued to eat and never offered any to the women. Watching him eat the food that was intended for them seemed to bolster their resolve, though they were extremely nervous.

It was a well-known fact that we never received any of the parcels sent by the Red Cross for the prisoners. We were so in need of those precious parcels, especially the disinfectants, painkillers, bandages, and ointments. The other items, such as powdered milk for the children, soap, chocolate bars, and assorted tins of food, would also have made an enormous difference in our lives. Prisoners working at headquarters had seen the contents of the parcels divided among the officers. We were sickened by the thought that they, who had plenty, were literally stealing our lives from us.

'Yes?' the commandant queried with his mouth full, looking the three women up and down with a leer.

Before she could lose her nerve, one of the women started to explain why they had come. Maybe something could be worked out so that people could have more food and water? It would also be good for the whole camp if we could have access to the medical supplies that the Red Cross was sending for the prisoners. There would be fewer deaths, and everybody would be happier.

She was staring helplessly at the parcel on the table, unaware that the commandant had stopped stuffing himself with the chocolates.

Perspiring profusely, his little glittering eyes never left her face as he stood up and reached for a bell. The two women at her side simultaneously reached over to her to silence any further speech. Hearts pounding, they realized they were in deep trouble.

The door flew open, and several guards marched in, their rifles raised and bayonets pointing at the women, waiting for instructions.

Slowly, ever so slowly and deliberately, the commandant walked around the women in ever-tightening circles, then he stopped and stood behind them for several minutes. It was as though he were considering what cruel punishment would give him the most satisfaction. To the women, it was an agonizing eternity. Hardly daring to breathe, they stared straight ahead and tried to anticipate his next move. They were unprepared, however, for what happened.

The commandant screamed out an order. Three of the guards rushed forward and dragged the women from the room and out the back door. There, in a little courtyard hidden from prying eyes, they received a horrible beating. Lashings from bamboo sticks across their bony backs sent them reeling to the ground. As they lay cowering in the dirt, trying to shield themselves from the brutal onslaught, army boots kicked viciously at their faces and ribs. With broken noses and teeth, and swelling eyes, the women tried to crawl away only to be pulled back by their hair. It came out by the handfuls. The guards, screaming obscenities, grabbed at their clothing until it ripped in their hands and left the women almost naked. And still they delivered more blows, even though there was no longer any resistance. The women were bleeding profusely as they lay curled up on the ground. The woman who had done all the talking happened to glance toward the door through which they had been hustled, and saw the squat figure of the commandant standing there. In his hand was the box of chocolates, from which he was calmly helping himself as he watched the beatings.

To keep any other prisoners from getting the idea that they could appeal to the Imperial Japanese Army, the three women were ordered to march around the entire camp for three days in the blazing sun, without food and water. To make absolutely sure we all understood that the Japanese army ruled supreme, every prisoner in the camp was denied their daily rations of rice and water for as long as the three women were on their march. To reinforce his point, the commandant ordered the next truckload of food to be dumped into a large dirt pit just outside the front gates. The pit was then filled with water and topped with more dirt.

Everyone was forced into the streets to take a good look at what could, and would, happen to anyone else with ideas about mercy.

My mother had no choice but to take us out to watch the horrific spectacle as the injured women slowly and painfully dragged themselves past us in the street. She tried to make us hide our eyes, but with children's natural curiosity, we peeked between our fingers and cried at what we saw. 'Are they going to die?' We begged to know. Hardly a thread of clothing covered them; their gaping wounds glistening in the broiling sun. Swarms of flies buzzed around their heads. Oozing pus and blood trickled down their arms and legs and caked the dirt on their unwashed bodies. Their arms hung limply at their sides as they shuffled, stooped over and heads down. Deathly silence followed their tortuous steps. By the third day, only one woman still dragged herself pathetically through the streets. She was almost crawling by this time. Fewer prisoners stood in the streets now to watch her go, as most of us no longer had the energy to do anything but stay on our beds. Here we quarreled and fought bitterly among ourselves. 'Get away! Don't touch me!' we cried in anger at the sibling lying by our side. We were so distraught by what we had witnessed, it was hard to tell whether the sickening cramps in our stomachs were from fear or hunger. Every last scrap of food was gone, and only a few mouthfuls of water were left in the bucket, which stood right next to the mattress now. We couldn't risk others helping themselves to it. Our mother tried hard to divert our attention by suggesting little games to play, but not many could ease our breaking spirits. I think she herself got through those difficult days by gazing at the painting on the wall. 'Don't you wonder what is hiding around the corner of that hill?' she would ask us. 'Look at that beautiful meadow where you can run and play.' She sounded almost wistful. 'Listen!' She held her finger up to her lips. 'Listen very carefully, children.' She pointed at the painting. 'I think I can hear *birds* singing in the flamboya tree.' We stared at her and then at the painting, with blank expressions. It was as though we had no feelings left.

———————

The three women somehow survived the terrible ordeal and were able to tell their story, but many prisoners could not make it through the days of starvation and drought. Their bodies were taken on a truck to be dumped in one of the communal graves outside camp.

The commandant was definitely achieving his goal.

———————

Though life was at its worst, and our mother knew there was nothing she could do about it, she was not going to allow us to give up. Once more she brought out the Children's Bible and paged through it till she found what she was looking for. She held it up so we could all see it, and we looked at the picture of Jesus surrounded by happy children and listened as she started to read. We knew the story well, but we never tired of hearing how much he loved us. Now more than ever we needed to hear again that 'each of us had a guardian angel in heaven.'

13

A Most Special Christmas

During those bleak days of hunger and senseless beatings, when our spirits were at their lowest, there came a moment so beautiful in its simplicity that I remember it to this day. It gave us the strength to continue, filled us with the hope that one day the war would be over and life would be better for all of us. A hopeful glimpse into the future.

It was Christmas Eve. Our third Christmas in the concentration camp, and though we had never actually been able to celebrate the holiday, it was somehow still a time for great excitement and anticipation. We listened in awe to the stories my mother told of wondrous trees all decorated with tinsel and baubles and starry lights. Trees that seemed to sparkle more with each year's telling. Our mouths watered at the thought of all those delectable treats reserved for Christmas, though we had no idea what they could possibly taste like. We saw in our mind's eye the flaming plum pudding, and were ready to dig into its imaginary center to retrieve the lucky charm that would make our dreams come true. Mince tarts, chocolate Saint Nicholases, tangerines, and nuts enjoyed in front of a crackling fire while the snowflakes fell silently outside the window. We had listened to those stories so many times that we could almost imagine ourselves living in that perfect setting. What could be more wonderful than Christmas Eve? Not even the sirens wailing in the distance or the rats scurrying around our feet could dampen our spirits this night.

'Stay very, very quiet. I won't be long.' She had smiled as she ushered us outside to wait until she was done. We knew we had to be watchful. We were listening to the *stomp, stomp, stomp* of the guards as they continued down the dirty road. The three of us, Willem, Gijs, and I, sat crouched behind a pile of discarded, bug-infested mattresses, not daring to breathe lest the guards return and find us there. It was difficult to keep Gijs quiet while we waited. He simply did not understand the importance of absolute silence when you were doing something forbidden, namely being out after curfew. He knew only that he was hungry and wanted something to eat, and he wanted it now.

Curfew had sounded long ago, forcing everyone inside, and all the blackout blinds were down. We did not know the reasons behind complete blackouts at night, as the guards never informed anyone about what was happening. We did know that if even the smallest crack of light showed through a window, one of the guards would barge into your room, half demented with anger, and whack at the light and anyone who got in the way. After we were liberated, we learned that Japan was losing the war at this time, and that the Allies were flying reconnaissance flights over the islands. Japan did not want the camps to be discovered. There were so many of them.

It was Christmas Eve, and the heavy blanket covered our little doorway completely. Behind that blanket, our mother was preparing Christmas! She had been acting mysterious all day, hinting at surprises.

We were snuggled close to one another, warm with excitement, when all of a sudden heavy boots came rushing down the street and stopped in front of the spot where we were hiding. It was one of the guards.

'Get inside!' he commanded. We froze in fear.

'Get inside! Now!' he screamed again. 'You know it is forbidden to be outside at this time of night!'

He must have seen us, I thought, but how could that be possible? We were sitting so quietly in the pitch dark. Nervously, we peeked around the mattresses. In the dim light of his flashlight, we could just distinguish the little bent figure of Mrs. Linder, our elderly neighbor. She was holding something very carefully in both hands. She, not us, was the subject of his wrath.

'Please, it's Christmas Eve,' we heard her frail voice pleading. 'I made this soup for my friend as a surprise. She's ill. Please let me take it to her?' She took a few steps away from the guard.

'No friend. Get inside! Now!' This time he pressed his bayonet into her side. He jabbed so hard that Mrs. Linder lurched to the ground, and the precious bowl of soup shattered around her.

'Oh God, no! My soup. My lovely soup,' she cried as she crawled around amid the shards of the white bowl.

We felt terrible pity for this frail old woman who barely had the strength to stand up. Worst of all, the Christmas surprise for her friend was totally ruined. I looked at the fragments of china scattered on the ground.

Just like the rice bowl from this morning, I thought.

It was my job to stand in the rice line with our black pan to pick up our four meager portions of rice for the day. I hated that job, as I was the only child in a long line of women, but my mother was usually attending to the sewers during this time. The rice was supposed to be shared out equally according to the number of people in each family, but even I could see that the women fortunate enough to be the leader's friends always got more than their fair share. On this particular morning, though, there was a surprise. Because it was Christmas, someone could win the small white bowl that was used to scoop the rice. There was a nervous lurch of excitement in my stomach. If only I could win that bowl, I'd have a gift for my mother. I knew she'd love it so much. But I could never be that lucky.

The leader wrote a number on a slip of paper and popped it into the pocket of her shorts. Then she walked slowly down the line of excited women and listened to the numbers they blurted out. What if someone took my number? I didn't know too many numbers yet, and I was near the end of the line.

'Speak up, girl! What number do you want?' the leader shouted impatiently as she towered in front of me.

I grew flustered. 'Six,' I whispered. That's how old I was.

'That's been called. Another one!' she boomed. Fear made me suck my thumb.

'Come on. Come on. Hurry up, or I will pass.'

'One,' I blurted out. I couldn't think of anything else.

She pulled the slip of paper slowly from her pocket.

'Number one,' she said, and looked at me so disdainfully that I began to wish I hadn't picked the correct number.

Nervously, I made my way up the line behind her to collect my prize. Past the women who had lost, most of whom smiled at me. The leader thrust the bowl at me so forcefully that I almost dropped it, but deep inside, I felt proud.

I had overcome inhibitions and fear and not only guessed the correct number, but I had actually spoken up to a woman who always terrified me. I resented the fact that she gave her friends more than their fair share of food, but I felt helpless to do anything about it. Who was going to listen to a child? I didn't want her to know that I knew what was going on; she would short our ration still more. I didn't even tell my mother, as I knew she wouldn't hesitate to complain.

As I headed back to the garage with the pan of rice and the little white bowl balanced precariously on top of the lid, I was filled with the exquisite joy of knowing that I had a Christmas surprise for my mother. Just imagining her happy face made me smile. She was not home when I returned, as she was still working in the sewers, so I had a chance to hide the precious gift under a corner of the mattress until Christmas Eve.

And now, as my brothers and I sat huddled in the dark, waiting for the festivities to begin, we were at risk of losing our Christmas after all. Our mother, however, had heard the commotion in the street. She carefully pulled the blanket aside and urged us to come in without making any noise.

Our room was in darkness as we crawled through the doorway, and our mother hastily replaced the blanket. This made it stiflingly hot in the little room. The perspiration trickled down our faces, but we did not dare leave the doorway open for fresh air. Our mother was busy in the dark, and though we strained our eyes, we could not make out exactly what she was doing. The episode of the soldier and Mrs. Linder had unnerved us. The heat inflamed the prickly rash all over our bodies and we couldn't stop scratching ourselves. Gijs was just starting to whimper when our mother struck a match and lit a small white candle standing in the middle of our crate table. Instant silence. The soft, flickering light had miraculously transported us from a dank dark corner of a garage to a place where Christmas still happened. It reflected off our tin plates into smiling faces and shining eyes full of wonder.

Twigs and grasses and different kinds of leaves lay scattered over our little table as decoration. We crawled breathlessly to our places and stared at the surprises next to our plates. A handwritten book for Willem, filled with adventure stories to encourage him to read. She had been writing them down for weeks on any papers she could find in the supplies we had brought with us. For Gijs, a big blue elephant with flowered ears, hand-sewn from one of her old dresses. And for me, a baby doll made from a sock and dressed in remnants of white tablecloth fabric. I loved the doll instantly.

'Merry Christmas, my darlings,' our mother whispered. In the excitement, I had almost forgotten the bowl, but swiftly I reached under the mattress and handed it proudly to her. As she stared at it in disbelief, tears welled up in her eyes, and I knew she loved it. She didn't have to say anything.

'Read Pappie's card to us again,' we begged her for the umpteenth time. It was the first piece of news we had received from him since we had entered camp, and it had arrived unexpectedly only days before. We were still very much under its spell. He was feeling fine, it said.

And he was sending us 'Much love and kisses for a cheerful Christmas.' We sat silently on the floor, entranced by the flickering candlelight on our small table and overcome by the utter joy of Christmas.

This prewritten card was the only news we received from my father during our war years in captivity. It came from No. 3 Branch Thai War Prisoners Camp in Nike, Thailand.

Suddenly, from the other side of the dividing curtain, soft singing arose: 'Silent night, holy night.'

It started as a whisper, ever so softly, then gradually increased in volume as our hearts gained courage through the magic of it all.

'Sing, children.' Our mother smiled.

Quietly we joined in, and then voices from each and every house up and down the streets took up the Christmas carol, until it sounded like the whole concentration camp was singing. It was indescribably beautiful and filled our hearts with a gladness we had not felt in a long, long time. I believe even the guards were affected, because it was one night they left the prisoners alone. There were no sirens or unexpected *tenkos*. No punishments for disturbing the peace. For one special and glorious moment, the war was forgotten, and it was truly Christmas. .

14

The Mungers

Every day now, when he had the energy, eight-year-old Willem had to go to work. Guards had been assigned to round up all seven- and eight-year-old boys and march them several miles out of camp to a work location. My mother's greatest fear was that Willem would one day not return. She knew that the ultimate plan was to rid the camp of as many boys as possible. If these long marches in the blazing sun did not kill the starving children, then the only alternative, the commandant thought, was to transfer them to one of the men's camps. The transfer age was originally fifteen. There were no more fifteen-year-olds in the camp, but there were still a lot of young boys wandering around. Obviously the transfer age had to be lowered again and again. It had now come down to the ten-year-olds. The petrified little boys were dragged screaming from their mother's weak arms and loaded into army trucks. The frantic mothers ran after the trucks crying that their sons were not old enough yet. 'They're still babies,' they wailed. 'How can they survive?'

All mothers of eight-year-olds cried with them, then rushed home to hold their own sons in their arms for as long as they could.

———

For the last few days, Willem and a handful of other little boys had been marched in the blazing sun to the commandant's house outside the camp. Here they were put to work picking up debris, raking gravel, or cutting the front lawn. It was a big lawn with a circular driveway and little shade.

The boys were told to spread out and were handed blunt kitchen knives to cut the grass. They had to grab a tuft of grass in one hand and hack away until all the blades of grass were cut, before moving on to the next tuft. It was backbreaking work in the full sun, without any breaks for food or water. Often the commandant watched their progress from his shaded porch, where he sat with his feet up on the railings. The boys left early in the morning, unless there was an unexpected *tenko,* and they usually returned around noon, before the heat became unbearable. This was not out of concern for the boys but because the guards themselves could not cope with the noonday sun.

Willem usually liked to go because it meant getting a little extra food at the end of the morning. It was nothing much, generally only a couple of slices of dry bread. It did not even taste that good, but any additional food, however paltry, was always welcome. Every day he would try hard to bring the slices home to share with us, and every day he had eaten them before he got back to camp. He would be so filled with remorse and shame that he could barely look us in the face. Then my mother would take him in her arms and hug him tightly to assure him that it was perfectly all right. She wanted him to eat what he had worked so hard for. He had earned it, after all. But his feelings of guilt were so great they stayed with him forever.

After one particularly grueling day, Willem came stomping home and threw himself angrily onto the mattress, hiding his face.

'What's the matter, Willem? Tell me! What happened?'

Our mother's voice was full of concern as she picked him up and looked into his face. What did they do to him, she wondered, checking him all over to see if he was hurt.

'It was so awful, Mummy,' he started as his eyes filled with tears. 'They made them kneel on the ground, and then –' He couldn't continue.

'And then what, darling?' She was so afraid of what he was going to tell her.

'Then the Japs grabbed all the ladies' hair and chopped it all off and threw it away. And the ladies were all crying. They wanted their hair back.' The words came tumbling out between heart-rending sobs. She threw her arms around his shaking little body, and her heart ached for her young son.

'And they were all laughing, Mum. The commandant and his friends were all laughing.' He hid his face against her shoulder.

'I know, darling. I know,' she whispered softly. How can you possibly explain sadistic behavior to a small boy? She knew about the hair-chopping incidents that the commandant enjoyed so much, especially when he was drinking and entertaining his friends. Any minor infraction was reason enough to bring a woman to his house to be punished as he saw fit. He hated Europeans, everybody knew that, and in his eyes this was a good way to bring more shame on these despised women. If they were lucky, the commandant would be too drunk and laughing too heartily to see that the women were hastily gathering and collecting as much of their shorn-off locks as they could. As soon as they got home, they would sew those locks carefully onto a scarf, which they would wear until their hair had grown back.

She felt furious that Willem had to witness such a cruel scene and decided to keep him home from now on. She would simply tell the guard that he was too ill to work. There were already many days when he did not have the strength to get up in the morning and make that long trek with the other boys, even for the few extra slices of bread. Tired and listless from lack of food, he preferred to stay home and sleep. Our food ration had been reduced yet again and was barely one small bowl of rice per day. Our bodies now looked like mere skeletons of skin over bone.

Willem's hands were also so blistered from the lawn work, and in such danger of becoming infected, that our mother wanted him home until they had time to heal. Open sores didn't heal easily anymore. We were already so covered in boils and tropical sores that we couldn't afford to take risks. My mother was always talking about the fact that all of us, but especially Willem, needed more protein in our diets. She was always worried about him.

None of us was a pretty sight. We were filthy, our scalps were covered with head lice, our teeth were black and rotten. Gumboils swelled our faces to the point that we could barely speak from the pain. When a large, pus-filled boil on my shoulder became so inflamed that the same woman who had pulled out my toenail had to lance it, I passed out on her table. I had simply run out of strength.

Though physical aches and pains had to be borne by us children, none could possibly have compared to the ache in our mother's heart. She, too, had heard the rumor called the Borneo Plan. Women were going to be shipped to Borneo to work in the mines, with so little food that they would soon collapse from starvation and die. Their children were to be left behind, either to fend for themselves in camp or to be scattered around Java, to be brought up by the natives who would not care in the least whether we lived or died. It sent chills through our mother's heart just to think of it. For days she kept us closely confined to our quarters and grabbed at any excuse not to send Willem out to work. What if he should be gone when she was taken away? She agonized over the question of how we were going to survive. She knew that we would surely die without her.

Time was running out, and the rumor became more of a certainty as each day passed. She knew she had to do something soon, but her plan was so dark and so utterly horrible, she didn't know how she was going to accomplish it. Would she be strong enough to carry it through to her last child? In her mind, it had come to the point that her children were going to die, either by her own hands as the ultimate act of love, or by slow and torturous starvation at the hands of our captors.

I know that she didn't like to talk about it, but she told me this story many years later. It still hurt her deeply to think about it. She said she knew what she had to do but not how to do it. She had already given the Japanese so much. Her home, her personal belongings, her beautiful garden, and her beloved music. She vowed she would never, ever give them her most precious possessions — her children. Timing was therefore crucial. If only she could find out when her name would be called. Would she have enough time to take care of her children? To do what she had to do? What if she carried out her plan and her departure was canceled?

The nightmare continued for days. She never let us out of her sight. We talked a lot about our father, whom we were starting to forget. We tried to imagine where he could be. What was he doing now? Was he thinking of us, too? Somehow my mother couldn't bring herself to think about a reunion anymore. A lot of time had passed. Three years, in fact. Three years of fear and hunger and pain. All that time she had clung to the belief that we would make it, but now she was not so sure. If she survived the work in the Borneo mines and was reunited with her husband, how could she tell him what she had done? She considered asking another woman without children to look after us until our father came to collect us after the war. Sad to say, she felt there wasn't anybody who would be committed for that long a time.

For days she paced the floor trying to find a solution. Stopping in front of the painting, she looked for solace there. Staring at the beautiful flamboya tree, she sighed and asked herself, 'Was there ever really such a peaceful life?'

There was no way around it, she realized. It was completely up to her. She grew so distraught she couldn't sleep at night. One mealtime she added her small portion of rice to our plates and sat and stared at us as we ate. We loved the extra food but sensed that something was terribly amiss.

'Why aren't you eating, Mummy?' we asked.

'Because I want you to have it,' she answered quietly, reaching over to squeeze our hands and stroke our faces. 'I don't need it anymore.'

――――――

Early the following morning, before we were properly awake, footsteps came running up the path and stopped just outside our entrance.

'Claar! Claar!' a voice whispered urgently into our room. Our mother jumped up, her face white with fear. Her heart thumping wildly in her chest, she stared at the shadow in the entrance. Oh my God, she thought, it must be today. The time has come. She was so numb with fear that she could hardly breathe as she stepped over us, still half asleep on the mattress.

'Claar, it's *over!*' The woman in the entrance was exuberant. 'We're not going! The Borneo Plan is canceled!' Our mother stared at her with blank, disbelieving eyes. Her legs were shaking. She felt confused. 'The Borneo Plan is canceled,' she repeated to herself several times. Slowly the meaning of those incredible words became clear in her mind. Her children had been spared. Life could go on.

'Are you sure?' she asked. The relief was so overwhelming

that our poor mother sank to the floor, covered her face with her hands, and cried.

———————

It was about this time, when it seemed things could not get much worse, that our lives were about to change. More rumors were circulating, but this time they hinted that the war was almost over. We had heard those rumors many times before. What was different this time was that we were now allowed visitors from the outside. We had seen new people coming in who were clean and nicely dressed, but we hadn't paid much attention to them. They hadn't come to see us. Who was out there, anyway, who would know where we were?

We had completely forgotten about the visitors when, one day, two strangers stood on the sidewalk in the shade, watching Gijs and me playing in the sand. They never said a word. They simply stood and stared at us with tears in their eyes.

When we could ignore them no longer, I looked in their direction and tentatively smiled.

'Claartje?' the woman said.

I stood up. 'Yes.'

'Oh, dear God. You don't remember us, do you?' The man and woman took a couple of steps toward us. 'We're the Mungers from Bandung. Remember? We took you to the hospital when your baby brother was born. Is this your baby brother?'

I looked at Gijs, his blond hair shining in the sun, covered from head to toe in dust and grime. I looked back at the Mungers. For the first time, I noticed the large cloth bags they were both carrying, bulging with wrapped packages of every size.

'Yes. That's Gijs, and my mother is in there.' I pointed to the back of the garage, to which we had eagerly returned to live as soon as it had become vacant again.

My mother and Willem were both lying down, as neither was feeling very well. The Mungers turned to look in the direction I was pointing, and then back at us, as though undecided about their next move. Then, with tears still streaming down their cheeks, they hurried up the driveway with their heavy bags. Gijs and I followed them with our eyes. Why were they crying?

The Mungers stopped outside the hole in the wall and peered into the darkness of our little room.

'Claar?' Mrs. Munger called hesitantly.

To our surprise, the Mungers and my mother rushed into one another's arms, crying loudly and clinging to one another as though they would never let go again. They sobbed and cried and laughed and cried some more.

Finally they moved inside, where more loud sobs could be heard. Gijs and I, by now unnerved by all this crying, simply stood by our sand pile and stared at the garage wall, trying to guess what was happening inside. When the crying subsided a bit and we could hear Willem's voice, too, we plucked up the courage to go see what all the upset was about.

We found everyone seated on the mattress, our mother holding tightly on to Mrs. Munger's hands with both of hers. The bags still stood in the middle of the room where they had been dropped. Three-year-old Gijs did not hesitate to go directly over and investigate the packages inside.

'Oh, yes,' Mrs. Munger said, 'I brought you some food. I thought you could probably use it.'

She could not possibly realize how wonderful those words sounded. She dragged the bags close and took out the wrapped packages. Chocolate, powdered milk, Spam, and eggs. Carrots, bananas, and a vanilla cake. Several bars of soap, toothpaste and brushes, and a jar of face cream for my mother. Tea and a bag of sugar, followed by packets of cookies. We couldn't believe what we were seeing. We simply sat and stared at everything in total silence.

Finally, our mother gave each of us children a cookie

and asked us to please go out and play so she could talk to her friends. We didn't want to leave, as this was much too interesting, so we sat down on the stoop outside the doorway to inspect the cookies in our hands. We sniffed at them and turned them over. We compared one another's as to size and color. We could hardly remember ever having eaten cookies before. It was Gijs who finally took a bite and then looked at the hole he had created in the side. Willem and I hesitated to take that first bite. Once it was eaten, we would no longer be able to anticipate how delicious it was going to be. Gijs munched happily on his until it was gone, then looked hopefully over to ours.

Inside the garage, the talking flowed without pause. There was so much to catch up on and deplore. The Mungers were disgusted with the living conditions in the camp and kept shaking their heads in disbelief. They had had no idea things were so bad. They wanted to help and wondered what they could do to improve our lives even a little. My mother didn't have to think twice about it. She begged them to smuggle Willem out of the camp, if it was at all possible. He was getting weaker and weaker every day, and she was desperately worried about him.

After much discussion, they had a plan. The Mungers told us that visitors were to be allowed into camp once a month. The next time they came, they would come in on bicycles, bring more food, of course, and then take Willem on the back of one of their bicycles as though he were their own son. It was very risky but worth a try.

The days that followed their visit were filled with anticipation. It was all we could talk about, quietly of course, only among ourselves. The food they had brought was a godsend and probably saved our lives. Each mealtime had a little something extra with it now. We were able to eat a cookie or piece of chocolate without feeling we had to save it for later. It was lovely to know that there would be more.

We were trying to get used to the idea that Willem would be leaving us. He was looking forward to a new adventure, but as the time approached for his departure, he became less and less certain.

The Mungers had measured him for clothes that they would buy and bring into camp so that he would not look so much like one of the prisoners.

More than anything, I wished I was going with him. I envisioned a pretty room with curtains at the windows and a soft bed with snowy white sheets, and I dreamed of eating vanilla cake all day long. How I loved vanilla cake! I would have sweet-smelling soaps for my bath and colored ribbons for my hair.

By the time the month was up and the Mungers arrived on their bicycles, I had made up my mind that I, too, would go with them to live a better life. Luckily for me, they brought up the possibility of taking me with them the next time they came for a visit. My mother wasn't so sure. She wanted to wait and see how it worked out with Willem. But I knew it would be just fine.

Throwing her arms around his bony shoulders, our mother hugged Willem tightly, not wanting to let him go. If only she could be certain that she was doing the right thing. To make matters worse, she could sense that Willem was feeling most unsure about leaving his family, though he would never admit it. Tenderly holding his face in her hands, she looked into his eyes and tried to impart to him that things were going to be all right.

'I'm going to miss you so very much,' she whispered as she kissed him good-bye for the last time. She hoped he couldn't see the tears in her eyes. She gave him last-minute instructions on how to behave as she helped him climb onto the back of the bicycle behind Mr. Munger. Lingering beside him as long as she could, she wondered if she would ever see her son again. She knew she had to go through with it because Willem was slowly starving to death. She prayed fervently that he would be safe and happy. She had cut his hair, and he was wearing the new shorts and shirt Mrs. Munger had brought. He even wore a brand-new pair of sandals. It was years since he had looked so respectable. Not at all like a prisoner. Our mother was sure the guards at the gate would be fooled.

She told Gijs and me not to stay out and wave in case we might inadvertently give something away. It could jeopardize any further visits.

We never told anyone that Willem had gone, mainly so we could still collect his small portion of rice each day, and also because we would be in serious trouble if the guards ever found out that a prisoner had actually escaped. By now they had become careless about counting heads, as so many prisoners died each day.

———

It was a long, agonizing month for my mother as she wondered whether they had made it out of camp safely. She hoped she had done the right thing. She was counting the days until the Mungers' next visit. What if they couldn't come? We missed Willem terribly and longed for news of him. My mother hoped and prayed that they had all gotten out all right, and that he had plenty to eat now. I tried to imagine what he could be doing other than eating a lot of delicious food. I hoped that Mrs. Munger would bring back a pretty red dress for me to wear, and red shoes to match.

While we waited for the Mungers' next visit, an unexpected event temporarily took our minds off Willem and escape. A *passar,* an open-air market, was allowed to take place inside the camp. We could only imagine that the natives wanted to be included in a possible moneymaking venture when they saw so many visitors carrying bags of food into the camp. We watched in fascination as natives swarmed in through the gates, pushing carts and wheelbarrows to the large central square. Bicycles, loaded with huge cloth bundles and baskets, overflowed with fruits and vegetables and precariously swayed from side to side on the way to the square. Colorful kiosks and tents sprang up wherever there was space. Beautiful batik fabrics, pottery, trinkets, and tin toys came out for display. Our eyes could hardly take it all in. Lovely as everything looked, however, none of the items caused as much unrest or anxiety as the food. Wandering past the stalls with my mother and Gijs, I wanted it all. Especially the little pastries. The pretty pink and white squares that oozed with syrup when you bit into them. We had just enough money to buy one. One small mouthful each. But the *passar* was going to be there the next day, and my mother promised I could come back for one more.

It was a long wait. My mother had her work to do in the sewers, so I had to watch Gijs till she got back. But I wasn't worried. Wasn't she always saying 'The first shall be the last, and the last shall be the first'? So confident was I that I would be the last at the pastry stall, and therefore the first, that I didn't hurry at all when my mother handed me some money. I even lingered at some of the other kiosks, as I had to make absolutely sure that I would be last. I could already taste the sweetness in my mouth and looked forward to that first bite. I couldn't delay any longer. Hurrying to the spot where I knew the table to be, I saw that it was empty. Bewildered, I looked around, and then I saw that the vendors were packing up and heading toward the entrance gates. What happened? Wasn't I first?

I felt crushed. My mother had lied to me. 'I wasn't first but last,' I screamed at her, in tears. At first she did not understand. Then, as she took me in her arms and tried to comfort me, she realized how confused I was about the Bible story of the poor beggar who would get to heaven before the rich and proud people. She was trying to teach us that it was more important to be kind and good than to be mean and in charge of other people, but it broke her heart that it had cost me my little cake.

The cake was soon forgotten when we saw Mrs. Munger come cycling up the road again. What a welcome sight she was, laden with bags on her carrier at the back. She started waving excitedly when she saw Gijs and me waiting for her.

She brought the good news that Willem had settled down well and looked a lot better with more food to eat. He was content to spend most days reading the endless supply of children's books that friends of the Mungers were bringing over for him. The only thing that concerned her was that he was so quiet, saying only a few words at most.

To my great disappointment, she had not been able to buy me the red dress and red shoes I had dreamed about, but had found me some pale green shorts and a blouse. She had also brought a pair of the most uncomfortable sandals I had ever worn. They became a matter of strife between us. I was always trying to lose them, as I really did prefer to walk barefoot. We never wore shoes in the camp anymore, as we had outgrown them all. The soles of our feet were hardened, like the feet of the

natives. But Mrs. Munger wouldn't hear of it. 'My goodness! All Dutch children wear shoes!' She assured me my
feet would get used to them very quickly.

With the disappointment of not getting a red dress
came feelings of extreme anguish as the time approached
for leaving my mother and Gijs. I squeezed as close to
my mother's side as I could while Mrs. Munger explained
what was going to happen and what I had to do. On no
account was I to look at the guards at the gate, or talk
to them. I had to pretend I did not understand what they
were saying. Mrs. Munger would speak to me in Swiss
German, and I would speak to her in Dutch.

The guards would never know the difference and
would believe that I was her daughter. It was a pretend
game, and it didn't matter what we talked about, because
nobody would be able to understand us. We were playing
a joke on them, I was told. Did I think I could play that
game?

The time had come for me to leave. My mother held
me in her arms and told me how much she loved me
and how proud she was of me. Told me to be good and
give Willem her love. Then she hoisted me onto the back
of the bike where the bags had been and, gathering Gijs
in her arms, walked quickly back to the garage and disappeared inside.

The back of the bike was hard, and I clung tightly to the saddle as Mrs. Munger pedaled toward the gates. My heart pounding wildly, I looked back several times in hopes that my mother had changed her mind, but she was nowhere in sight.

I tried to remember everything I had been told. We joined a stream of people all headed in the same direction. The visitors carrying bags, empty now, were anxious to get out of camp and the filth and squalor that we prisoners had grown accustomed to. Most were on foot, having left their cars outside the barbwire fences. Some were on bikes but got off to push them when they neared the gates. Mrs. Munger got off, too, as it was difficult to steer between the walkers. She tried to stick close to the other people so that we would be in a crowd when we reached the guards. Everyone had to hold up their yellow visitors' cards before they could pass through. I could see that Mrs. Munger had two cards, one slightly hidden behind the other. We were moving slowly, and my legs were beginning to ache as they dangled on each side of the wheels. People were pushing past, and Mrs. Munger was struggling to keep the bike upright and hold the cards in view at the same time. It was extremely hot, and the dust kicked up by the many feet made us choke and cough. Bicycles held up the line, and the guards were becoming impatient.

'Lekas! Lekas!' they kept screaming as they tried to move
the line faster. From time to time Mrs. Munger turned
to me and spoke loudly in German. She got me so
confused I didn't say a word. When we reached the gates,
the guards didn't even inspect our cards, and we rushed
through to the other side. Mrs. Munger got back on the
bike and pedaled as fast as she could down the road and
out of sight of the camp. Even then she did not slow
down; she seemed fiercely determined to pass the natives
beside the road at high speed, as though she expected
trouble.

I did not know at that time just how much danger
we were in as we sailed past. Men would appear out of
nowhere with hostile looks on their faces. Some carried
heavy sticks or machetes. Apparently these same men
later became the guerrillas who would fight the Dutch
government in Indonesia to try to rid themselves of all
Dutch people. Who could be easier targets than the
women and children in these camps? They would start
right here. Once the war was over and Japan had capitu-
lated, there was nothing and no one to stop them from
getting all the ammunition and weapons they needed.
They simply helped themselves. I was unaware, until
much later, that many an escapee from camp had met
an unfortunate end at the hands of these natives.

For the time being, however, I was extremely grateful when we finally reached the little dirt alley where Mrs. Munger had parked her car and I could jump off the bike. I don't know how long we had been riding, probably just an hour at the most, but it felt so wonderful to stretch my legs again that all I wanted to do was skip around and jump over the grass at the side of the path. With an anxious glance around, Mrs. Munger quickly pushed me into the backseat of the car, then lifted the bike into the trunk. Slamming it closed, she jumped in behind the steering wheel and turned to lock all the doors. Wasting no time, she reversed the car into the road and sped off as fast as she could toward her home in another part of Bandung. Not until then did she relax.

It felt wonderful to ride in a car again. I had forgotten how exciting it could be. Pressing my face to the window, I tried to recognize where we were going. Impossible. It had been three years or more, and what the Japanese army hadn't destroyed, the bombs had finished off. From time to time I saw Japanese soldiers sauntering beside the road, and my heart would skip a beat. I hunkered down in the backseat to hide my face. What if they should see me outside of camp? I wished Mrs. Munger would turn around and take me back. I knew I was in for a lot of trouble. Oh, if only my mother were here.

Mrs. Munger tried her best to reassure me. Weren't we pretending that I was her daughter? The soldiers wouldn't dare touch us. Swiss people weren't included in the war. It was hard to understand, but she didn't seem at all afraid. I just hoped we would arrive at her house soon.

After what seemed like hours, Mrs. Munger miraculously produced a packet of sandwiches and fruit. At first I simply sat and stared at the sandwich. White bread was something new to me. It was so soft and clean-looking that I thought it must be cake. I tucked some of it into the pockets of my shorts. You never knew what was going to happen. It was always better to keep some for later.

———

I was fast asleep in the backseat when we finally arrived at her house several hours later. I awoke to tapping on the car window and saw Willem's smiling face. He was so happy to see me again, he couldn't wait to ask me all about our mother and Gijs and what was happening in camp. Then he dragged me into the house, anxious to show me the room we would be sharing. There were two enormous beds next to each other, with a nightstand between. The shutters had been closed across the tall windows all day, so it was lovely and cool in the room. At the far end, a door led into the bathroom. It was hard to imagine we had a bathroom all to ourselves. Everything was so incredibly white and clean. I crept around the room, not really daring to touch the shiny porcelain, until Willem reached over and, smiling broadly, turned on the tap.

Just to see that crystal-clear water cascading into a sparkling clean basin brought forth giggles of delight. Who could have imagined such luxury? And that was for Willem and me to share? Unbelievable!

I had taken off my uncomfortable sandals and was enjoying the cool of the tiles on my sore feet when Mrs. Munger came into the room. She noticed my bare feet immediately and ordered me to put my shoes back on. 'It's much too dangerous,' she said, 'to walk about without shoes. There is so much dirt around, and bugs and ants that could sting.'

I looked down at the floor. Compared to the dirt we lived with every day in camp, this place seemed like heaven to me.

Mrs. Munger asked us to follow her into the living room, where a small white poodle lay cowering under a table. Not too far away from it sat an enormous German shepherd. He was watching every move the other dog made and barked ferociously whenever the poodle sat up or moved from its spot.

Willem held me back so I wouldn't move too close to the bigger dog.

'Oh, Hector! You are so bad,' Mrs. Munger said as she lovingly stroked the big dog on the head. She explained to me that she had gotten the poodle only a couple of weeks earlier and that Hector was not used to having another dog in the house. He was very jealous of the poodle.

'And that reminds me,' she said, looking straight at me, 'I'd like you to walk slowly and calmly across the room in front of Hector, so that he can get used to you, too.'

I stared at Hector and shrank back in horror, but Willem reached over and held on to my arm. 'Do it,' he whispered. 'I did it, too, and now he knows me.'

Willem confided to me later how terrified he had been because he had had to do it all alone. He offered to go with me, so we walked together, side by side, back and forth in front of Hector. It took all my willpower not to dash out of the room. Most of the time the big dog ignored us, only occasionally stretching his neck to sniff at us as we passed. I just hoped he was not able to see my shaking legs or hear my pounding heart. The poor poodle, on the other hand, never got the chance to make friends with the bigger dog. It was so nervous that it often soiled in the house. One day when it was being punished for this misdemeanor, Hector rushed up and grabbed the poor poodle by the neck, shaking it until it screeched in pain and anguish. This mean act simply confirmed my fear that Hector was not to be trusted. I felt as frightened of that big dog as the poodle did.

It was Mr. Munger who finally decided to find a better home for the poodle. I was greatly relieved.

Though they didn't have a very big garden, the Mungers also kept chickens. It was the eggs from those chickens that they had brought to us in the camp. One day Hector managed to get into the coop and killed several of the chickens. It was a mess, with blood and feathers everywhere. To my surprise, Mrs. Munger didn't get too angry. 'That is what dogs do,' she explained, but it just made me more scared of him. She took this opportunity to show me what was inside one of the chickens that Hector had ripped open: the heart and liver, and the long orange-colored tube that contained the tiny eggs that the chicken would eventually lay, one at a time. She used many of the eggs to make my favorite vanilla cakes, she told me.

Apart from eating, there wasn't much to do during the

day. It was not a good idea to roam around, and Mrs. Munger never let us out of her sight. Willem and I were still worried that a Japanese soldier would spot us outside the camp. The Mungers had no children of their own, so they weren't used to our ways. We were not to make noise or rush about. We had to stay spotlessly clean and definitely had to keep our shoes on. A couple of times we did venture out to one of the larger stores in Batavia with her, and she bought us some more clothes, but otherwise we simply stayed inside and tried not to get in the way.

At first things didn't seem too bad. It was so wonderful not to feel those angry, gnawing pangs of hunger in my stomach all day. But it didn't take long for those hunger pangs to be replaced by a terrible aching in my heart to go home. I became dreadfully homesick for my mother and our little corner in the garage. I would think of her all day long and tried to imagine her as she went about her day.

Nighttime was the worst. As soon as the lights were turned off, the fear of never seeing my mother or Gijs again would so upset me that I would cry myself to sleep. To add to my chagrin, I started wetting the bed in my sleep. I was no better than the poodle, I decided. I knew how Mrs. Munger felt about cleanliness, and I tried to get to the bathroom in time, but I was always too late.

My mother used to get us up at night, so it was seldom a problem in camp.

I tried to persuade Mrs. Munger to take me back to camp since I was always wetting her bed, but she said she would have to think about it. She wanted me to try really hard to get up in time. I desperately wanted to please her. In my mind, a dry bed became a ticket back to camp and my mother. It seemed such an impossible task, though. Much as I tried, I continued to wet.

The only way I was going to stay dry, I reasoned, was to stay awake. I tossed and turned and tried to keep my eyes open. The room was so dark. A couple of times I dozed off and woke with a start. With a thumping heart, I felt around the bed. Thank goodness, still dry, but I had to go so badly. And I was scared. Very scared. The room was so dark. I knew I had to be brave to make it over to the light switch just inside the door. I could already imagine how pleased Mrs. Munger was going to be when she found out in the morning that I was still dry. Gathering up all of my courage, I got up and slowly groped my way around the bed, straining my ears for any strange noises, and felt my way along the wall where the light switch was located. One more step and the light would be on. Everything was going to be all right after all.

As I stepped forward and reached for the switch, however, I felt myself rise into the air on something warm and furry that growled and barked and sent me tumbling across the floor. The commotion brought the Mungers running into the room. When the light came on, Hector was standing over me, sniffing at the puddle I was lying in. In total humiliation, I tried to cover my face with my arms. I can't remember ever feeling so dejected. And things didn't get any better. I couldn't sleep well at night because staying dry had become such an important issue to me and I was so unsuccessful at it.

Also, hard as it may be to believe, I had lost my appetite. I was so homesick, and the pain of separation from my mother was so great, I could no longer eat even my favorite vanilla cake. It had come to the point that no amount of persuasion or cajoling by an anxious Mrs. Munger could get me to eat.

At long last, and after much deliberation, it was decided that I should be returned to the camp. Willem begged me not to go, but I couldn't listen even to his pleas. All I could imagine was my mother's face, happy to see me again.

There was a lot to organize before we could leave. Bags of food to pack. Soaps and medicines. Visitors' passes to obtain. At the last moment it was decided that Willem should return, too, as there had been rumors that many of the prisoners were to be moved to different camps. We did not know who, where, or why, but we certainly would not want to lose touch with our mother.

To me, the return trip was a lot less stressful than the trip out. All I could think of was that I was going home at last. Mr. Munger was with us this time. He drove the car. The bikes were in the trunk, and the bags of food sat between Willem and me on the backseat. Again we had been instructed not to say a word when we arrived at the camp gates. We were just visitors going in to visit some friends of ours. Once more, the car was parked in a little alley, and then the bikes were loaded with great speed. Willem and I sat on the carriers each holding a heavy bag filled with food and other necessities. I didn't care in the least how heavy the bag was. I was nearly home, and that was all that mattered.

It was not nearly as difficult to get into the camp as it was to get out. The huge wooden gates stood wide open, with only a few disreputable-looking soldiers roaming about in front of the guardhouse. The Mungers held up their passes without even stopping their bikes. The soldiers looked up and simply waved us on. Now I could hardly sit still. I kept trying to peer around Mrs. Munger's derriere while hanging on to the heavy bag on my lap. I was already imagining how happy our mother was going to be when we suddenly appeared before her. There had been no way to let her know we were returning. Several times I looked over to Willem, but he was so intent on finding his friends that he never noticed me.

All of a sudden we were there. Back at our squalid, bug-infested, dank little corner of the garage. The place I had longed for and dreamed about for so many days. To me, no sweeter sight could be imagined than my mother running clumsily toward us on her swollen legs, her arms opened wide for a welcoming embrace when she realized it was us. The bicycle had hardly stopped before we were in each other's arms. It felt so good to be home at last that I didn't want to let her go. She had not been expecting us back so soon but hoped every day to somehow receive word that we had made it out safely. Our departure had left a terrible void in her life. Though she hoped deep down in her heart that she had done the right thing, she couldn't help feeling guilty in case things had gone wrong. Had she put us at great risk for nothing?

Our absence had not been easy to hide, either. She was still collecting our portions of rice, though people were starting to ask questions. Where were we? Were we ill? She tried to avoid long conversations and never told Gijs where we had gone. At three years old, he could not yet keep secrets.

There was another worry, too. More and more stories were flying around that people were being moved. That maybe the war was over. What if she was moved and lost contact with us?

Now, thank God, we were back, and she could not keep her eyes off us. She realized how much she had missed us, and made up her mind that whatever happened from now on would happen to all of us. Life was so uncertain, she felt, that the only thing she could be sure about was that the four of us belonged together.

15

Journey to Bangkok

August 1945, and most of the world was celebrating the end of the war. Not so the concentration camps. We knew nothing. Of course, we hoped the Japanese were losing the war. The only indication that something was happening at last had been when the visitors were allowed to enter. Also, we were subjected to fewer *tenkos*. This was wonderful, and everyone began to speculate about a possible end to all the misery we had been enduring, but nobody dared give in completely to their feelings of hope. In spite of the guards' reluctance to enlighten us, there was a definite uplifting of spirits in the camp, a feeling of excitement in the air. After all these years of hopelessness, we clung desperately to any hint of deliverance.

Unfortunately, our troubles were far from over. An immediate and almost more severe danger lurked just outside the barbwire fence in the form of the native guerrilla fighters.

The convenience of having all the women and children confined in one location made annihilation of the weakest that much simpler. The guerrillas hoped that hand grenades tossed over the barbwire fences, or sniper fire from convenient locations in the hills overlooking the camps, would decrease the Dutch population and bring the beginning of self-rule. They knew the women and children could not fight back.

Under the terms of their surrender, Japan was responsible for the welfare of all the prisoners in the concentration camps until the Allies arrived to take us all to safety. The commandant was immediately captured by the British and moved to a high-security prison in Batavia. He was later brought before the Batavia Military Tribunal and charged with carrying out the most inhumane and cruel treatment of prisoners. He was condemned to death and executed by firing squad in 1946. He was thirty-six years old.

With his removal, the Japanese guards no longer cared

what happened to anyone. They didn't even care enough to help one of their own when he was brutally attacked by dozens of women prisoners who had finally had enough of his cruel and sadistic behavior. We heard how the women hurled rocks and stones at the soldier with as much force as they could muster in their weakened condition, while the guards simply stood and looked on. It was as though everyone had suddenly gone mad. More and more women and children started running toward this scene, urging others to follow. You could not help but get caught up in the excitement, and we children were ready to run with them.

Not for one instant did our mother's resolve to protect us from all brutality, whether against us or the enemy, waver. She demanded we come immediately into our room, then sat us down and quietly talked to us about good and bad and staying out of trouble. She realized just how dangerous life had become for us.

I do not know exactly how much time passed between the end of the war and our finding out that it was over. I believe it was several months. The women's camps were so well hidden and so spread out over the islands that it took the Allies quite some time to find all of us. It was during this waiting that we had to contend with the guerrilla sniper attacks, and we really began to fear for our lives. It seems ironic that we could have made it this far only to lose our lives when the war was over. Nobody tried to barter through the fence anymore or in any way contact those on the outside. We tried to stay well away from the fences and as hidden from view as possible.

Our lives were now so focused around being rescued that when the Allied trucks finally came rumbling over the rutted roads, everyone heard them almost simultaneously and rushed en masse to the front gates, thrilled to welcome these British heroes with open arms. This time, even our mother, with us running eagerly beside her, joined the exuberant throng.

The British had brought plenty of food with them, which they distributed immediately, with promises of much more to come. They also brought the news we had all been waiting so anxiously to hear – the war was well and truly over. The Japanese had lost. There were cheers, as well as tears and smiles and hugs. Children rushed around in noisy groups, and everyone started dancing in the streets. But the big question on everyone's lips was 'Now what?'

The British told us that we would be moved to Bangkok as soon as possible, as it was definitely not safe here. We would go to a holding station until we could find transportation back to Holland. It was going to be wonderful in Bangkok, we were told. Nice, clean living conditions, more food, proper bathrooms, doctors, and shops where we could buy clothes.

A flurry of excitement swept into everyone's lives. We started packing. What was there to pack? All of the sheets and tablecloths my mother had brought at the beginning of the war were gone, used to make clothes for us or traded for food and medicine. The bottles of cod-liver oil were long gone. All that remained were the few tins we used as cups and plates, our black rice pan, and the clothes we were wearing. The mattress was so riddled with bed lice, we would be very happy to leave that behind. Anyway, we were promised beds to sleep on in Bangkok, in our own little room. It was something dreams were made of.

Our few pathetic belongings all fit into one small suitcase, including the painting of the flamboya tree, which, in all our years in camp, had miraculously never been touched by the guards.

Now, early each morning, we packed that suitcase and dragged it out to the roadside in front of the house, where we eagerly waited for the truck that would take us away from this hated camp forever. We had been looking forward to this day for weeks, months, years. We would be moved in alphabetical order, they said.

The wait turned out to be almost unendurable. The days came and went, and still the trucks had not come. Was something wrong? Had they forgotten about us?

My mother tried to busy herself with little tasks to pass the time. Since we children wouldn't leave our place on top of the suitcase at the side of the road, she came out to us armed with the tattered old Children's Bible and read us the same old familiar stories we had been reading all the years we'd been here. The words were so familiar by now that we could almost recite them by heart. But out there on the suitcase, we were not interested in listening to any more stories. Our ears were tuned to heavy trucks, and our eyes scanned the streets for any signs of their appearance. We would not leave our post for fear the trucks would arrive and we would not be there.

At night, long after the sun had gone down and the mosquitoes were out, we dragged that suitcase forlornly back into the garage and flopped down once more on our filthy mattress without bothering to unpack. 'It's just not fair!' I cried as I beat the mattress with my fists. 'I don't think they're ever coming back for us, and I don't care anymore,' Willem screamed. Angry tears streaked down our faces as we tried to swallow the dry, lumpy rice that our mother coaxed us to eat. Her face looked grim and she seldom smiled. 'They *will* come back. I promise you,' she assured us. She tried to sound optimistic as she rocked Gijs gently back and forth. He lay listlessly in her lap, staring into space. She didn't like to admit it even to herself, but she was beginning to wonder if we were going to make it until the trucks came back.

A lot of our friends had already gone to that better life in Bangkok, and we were forgotten, we were sure of it. The last of our energy had been used up in the excitement of liberation. We could manage only a small measure of exuberance when we congratulated friends whose time had come. We would help them onto the trucks and pass up their meager possessions as they promised to look for us in Bangkok. 'See you soon,' they called happily, and disappeared in a red cloud of dust. Our hopes and fears went with them. Several weeks later, here we were, still in the same filthy conditions, but with one enormous difference: We had pretty much lost hope.

We were not the only ones, by any means. There were hundreds of prisoners wandering aimlessly around camp. The Japanese soldiers no longer paraded up and down the streets. They were mostly congregated in the former headquarters, smoking, drinking tea, or simply dozing in the shade of the trees. *Tenko* was a thing of the past. With the end of the war, all rules and regulations fell apart, and life became almost more difficult than before. For a while it looked as though there would be no one to do the cooking or regulate food distribution, and fights had become the only way to settle differences. Lucky, maybe, that everyone was too weak to really hurt one another when a brawl broke out.

Though the heavy gates into the camp were no longer locked, nobody ever tried to leave. The outside world, it appeared, was not ready to welcome us. The Indonesians who lived around the perimeter had, in our four years of imprisonment, learned to resent and hate us. They could not tolerate us walking about on their side of the barbwire fence. It was rumored that several people had recently been stabbed to death when they had set foot outside the camp. Most prisoners had decided to wait it out. After all, what were a couple more weeks after nearly four years?

———

The day our truck finally arrived, we almost missed it. We were no longer watching for it. For over a week now, we had not dragged our suitcase to the side of the road. The days had been so excruciatingly hot, we had spent most of the time simply lying around on the mattress, dozing or staring out the doorway at the haze of heat shimmering on the rooftop. The only reason to get up once a day was to collect our portion of soggy gray rice and carry it back to the garage.

It was still very early in the morning, but already our perspiring bodies felt glued to the mattress where we lay. Willem had gone out to check if there was any water trickling out of the tap at the end of the driveway. He would collect in our bucket whatever was flowing, to be rationed over the course of the day. If you did not get there early enough, it simply dried up, and you would have to go without for the rest of the day.

It was while Willem was sitting there waiting for the bucket to fill that he first heard it. The laborious crunching and grating of heavy gears. He listened carefully, then, jumping up, he tore into the garage.

'The truck! The truck!' he screamed. 'It's coming! Get up!'

He tore out of the garage again and back to the road. My mother scrambled up as fast as she could, shouting instructions for us to throw everything into the suitcase. By this time we heard it, too. The loud rumble of the engine and the clanging of the metal benches as they shook and rattled over the potholes in the road.

Willem was waving his arms for us to hurry, and dashing into the street as if, with his skinny little body, he was going to prevent the advancing fleet of trucks from passing us by. He was almost crying in his frustration at our slowness. Gijs stood in the middle of the garage bawling his eyes out, terrified that he was going to be left behind. Grabbing the suitcase in one hand and Gijs with the other, my mother rushed us down the driveway for the last time.

We never once looked back.

The truck made frequent stops along the way, picking up as many prisoners as possible. There seemed to be no organized limit as to how many people could climb on board. Ours was not the only truck with people hanging over the sides or sitting on the fenders. Sometimes precious bundles were simply tossed overboard to make room for people desperate to leave this camp behind forever. Luckily for us, we were seated on our small case. Otherwise it, too, would have ended up on the dusty roadside.

The trucks were again manned by British soldiers. Though we could not understand a word they were saying, they exuded confidence and authority. No Indonesian or Japanese soldier was going to give us any trouble, we could see that. A large machine gun mounted on the roof of the cab was pointed at the side of the road. At any hint of trouble, a couple of warning rounds could be shot into the bushes. The British soldiers carried with them huge amounts of food. Big loaves of bread, cheese, fruit, and chocolate bars. Having forgotten our manners, we grabbed for anything they handed out, and greedily choked it down. How kind their faces were, and how full of concern. We must have been quite a sight.

For what seemed like several hours, the convoy of trucks crawled along the sandy roads in the blazing sun until we arrived at the river where a boat was waiting to take us to Bangkok. It was not a big boat, and when all the prisoners had filed on board, it was filled to capacity. We had hoped to get a space inside so we could get out of the sun, but it was so full in there, they couldn't even get the doors open anymore. We found a tiny space on the back deck. Gijs had to sit on my mother's lap, while I squeezed in next to her. Willem preferred to stand; as a nine-year-old, he was fascinated by all the activities on board. Every little space was taken up by people. We were so overcrowded that the boat lay very low in the water as we chugged slowly up the red, muddy river in the blazing sun. Those who passed out from the heat simply stayed upright, held up by their neighbors on either side.

There was very little water on board, and unless you had brought your own, practically no food, either.

Just when we thought things could get no worse, the unimaginable happened. Willem had managed to squeeze between the people on deck and had made his way to the front of the boat. There he stood in the point of the railing, wedged in by the people around him. Several people were sitting on the railing with their legs dangling over the side. Nobody was saying much. The unrelenting sun continued to blaze down, its white rays reflecting off the dirty water.

Suddenly, an earsplitting explosion blew our quiet world apart. In a cloud of darkness, we became a tangle of squirming bodies desperately trying to grab on to anything that would prevent our falling into the unknown. Through choking black smoke, we screamed and gasped for air, slipping out of control along the deck of the boat. The windows had shattered all around us, and the doors were blown out. The back of the boat rose into the air, and the front was slipping under the water. Then, with a tremendous splash that sent waves of filthy water crashing over the deck, the boat righted itself again and floated down the river. People crawled over one another, desperately trying to find children and relatives before we sank.

We had narrowly escaped being blown up when debris, stirred up by our boat's propeller, had been forced against a submerged mine. Willem, in the front of the boat, had been totally underwater and pinned in place by the bodies falling against him when the back went up. He appeared now, covered in mud and twigs and garbage, but such a welcome sight. We thought we had lost him.

The air was filled with screaming and crying women for whom this experience was the last straw. It seemed their sanity had finally snapped, and they continued to scream or cry for the rest of the day.

The dark smoke covered us all with a thin layer of tissuelike flakes that crumbled to nothing when you touched them, and the acrid smell of burning followed us for miles down the river.

It was early evening of the third day when our boat finally limped into Bangkok. A straggly bunch of dirty, soot-covered prisoners staggered off the gangplank. Exhausted, hungry, and dehydrated, we could barely make it to the waiting trucks. Dutch soldiers, who had been awaiting our arrival to transport us to the camp, brought buckets of water and cups. They waited patiently while we drank our fill. No water ever tasted so sweet.

Then, refreshed and spirits uplifted by the Dutch soldiers, we found the strength to climb up into one more truck. The soldiers explained that they were assigned to guard the camp while the women and children waited for transportation back to Holland. This was incredible news. Everyone started talking at once. Women were calling out names of husbands or sons. Were they here? Did the soldiers know their whereabouts? How long had they been here? What was happening in the rest of the world? Everyone on the truck was starved, not only for food but for news of their families. My mother was registering at the guardhouse just inside the gates.

'Are you absolutely sure?' she asked the guard inside the little house, her voice incredulous. She listened in stunned silence to his reply as we crowded around her.

'Who is here?' we wanted to know as she continued to stare at the guard. We pulled on her arm to get her attention. 'Who is here?' we asked again.

'*Pappie* is here. He is *here,* in this camp,' she answered breathlessly as she tugged at her rumpled shorts and combed her fingers through her dirty hair. 'What must I look like?'

16

Margriet Kamp

As we waited impatiently to finish registering, we had plenty of time to study our new surroundings.

The first major improvement was the absence of barbwire. What a relief! The woven bamboo fencing surrounded the whole camp, but this was obviously for protection, not to keep us confined.

The housing was also different. Instead of regular homes that had been confiscated from their owners, as in the previous camp, these were large wooden barracks, two or three stories high. They had probably been used previously as housing for soldiers. The barracks enclosed two sides of the camp and overlooked a large grassy area.

The third side of the camp bordered a busy, wide, and dirty river. The river was so full of sailboats, houseboats, and sampans, you could have moved right across it by jumping from boat to boat. For the Thai people, the river was their life. It was their drinking water, bathing water, and the place where all sewage was dumped. On a hot, humid day, which was most days, you could smell that river for miles around.

The last fence was the front of the camp, with an entrance gate and the guardhouse where we all had to register. Little shops ran along the outside of this fence. Some of them even had entrances leading from the camp through a back door into the shop. Most of the time, though, these back entrances were locked. No matter. To all of us waiting in line, it looked wonderful. We couldn't wait to get settled.

We were soon assigned a small room on the top floor of one of the rambling wooden barracks. Unfortunately, it was right under the tin roof. During the heat of the day, it was impossible to stay in that room without passing out. The temperature got so high it was like living in an oven. We spent all our days outside, under the trees, and in the evenings we would gather with other families on the grassy area in front to eat dinner and wait until our rooms had cooled off. It was a great time for storytelling and counting the stars in the sky. We watched for shooting stars and made hundreds of wishes, fully believing they would come true now. The star most wished upon was, of course, the one that would take us safely back home to our families in Europe.

When it was time for bed, we felt our way up the stairs in the dark, as there was no electricity. Canvas army cots had been set up around the walls in each room. After sleeping for years on a hard mattress on the floor, it was difficult to get used to a bed that curved up around you and was so narrow you couldn't curl up on your side.

My father lived for a short time with us in this room. It was probably as hard for him to get used to as it was for us. It seemed strange to me that even though we were all in the same camp, we saw so little of him. It had been an incredible surprise for my parents when they discovered they were in the same camp. He had been assigned, probably by the Dutch army, to help protect the women and children until transportation to Holland could be found for them. For weeks he had been checking the lists of prisoners arriving from the women's camps, and had almost given up hope that he would ever see us again when we suddenly appeared. Willem and I hardly knew him anymore, after almost four years away, and Gijs had never known him, having been born after the Japanese soldiers had taken our father away. My mother had to introduce them when we arrived at the camp and our father asked her, 'Who is this child?' He had obviously forgotten that she was pregnant when he was taken away by the Japanese at the start of the war.

Apart from the army cots, there wasn't much else in our assigned room. Nails on the walls held our few items of clothing, and a small table under the only window was storage space for the tin plates and cups we'd brought with us. Though the window lacked glass panes or shutters, the room was so dismally dark and airless we could barely make out the shape of the flamboya tree where it hung on the wall.

'This room is only good for sleeping in,' my mother said wistfully.

She never complained, though she must have been terribly disappointed. She had had high hopes of better living conditions in Bangkok. True, the food was a little more plentiful and varied, but our living quarters left a lot to be desired. I remember waking up one night to find myself lying in a deep puddle of water that had collected on my cot. I was convinced that I had wet myself while asleep but was amazed at the amount. My hair, my shoulders, everything was soaked. I was so disgusted with myself that I jumped down off the cot. Then I saw that my mother was already up and trying to pull all the army cots into the middle of the room.

'The rains,' she whispered, and then I heard it, too. The monsoons had started, and the rain was hammering on the tin roof and pouring in through the cracks. There wasn't a dry spot anywhere.

There was nowhere for us to go to stay dry. There were no other rooms, and every family on the top floor was facing the same problem. This was an old building, and the rusty roof had not been repaired in many years. We would have to stick it out for the duration of the rainy season, three to four more months.

With any luck, we would be on our way before long. We were all suffering from malnutrition. The food had not improved much; it was the same old rice, though we did get more vegetables and fruit. It was almost too late, as our stomachs could hardly handle anything but rice at this point. We were all still suffering from amoebic dysentery, and the fruit just made the diarrhea worse.

Unfortunately, this contributed to the death of many more prisoners. We were so weak and sickly that we caught any disease going around. Every day was a struggle for my mother. Her swollen legs shook and wobbled with every step she took, and her thick calves draped over her callused feet. There had been cases in camp, we were told, where the beriberi had become so severe that the fluid under the skin had burst through and caused death. It was a fear we children lived with every day, though our mother assured us this was not true and it was not going to happen to her.

Her health was deteriorating so rapidly it was almost as though she had lost the will to live. We kept her going, she told us many years later. She was so determined to bring us safely back to Holland that she repeatedly told us stories about fun in the snow and skating on frozen canals. It was hard to imagine what that could be like, all the white snow falling from the sky. I believe she instilled in us this longing to see Holland just to give us all something to look forward to.

I think that within her innermost self, our mother had come to the realization that her husband was not the man she had said good-bye to four years earlier. She did not know whether the distance between them was the result of the inhuman treatment he had suffered at the hands of the Japanese, or if there was someone else in his life. She knew only that her hopes for a happy reunion were not to be. He was never there to give her support or to take some of the responsibility of caring for his children in this new camp. It was strange, but we never relied on him for anything. It was as though we sensed their tension, and we felt quite relieved that he seldom slept in our little room with us. Guard duty kept him busy for long hours and most often well into the night. On those occasions he preferred to sleep in the officers' quarters.

———

The years of deprivation had made everyone feel hopeless and bitter, and we found it hard to believe that there really was a better life ahead. We were now so used to being dirty and malnourished, we couldn't even remember how it used to be. Our bones stuck out, and our eyes looked hollow. Most women suffered from beriberi, and many of the children had painfully swollen faces from the gumboils that plagued us. Our teeth were rotting, and our bodies were still covered in open sores that would not heal. Where were the doctors we were promised in Bangkok?

In spite of everything, it was not as difficult for us children as it was for the adults. We didn't know any better.

———

There was one major improvement in our lives: the bathing facilities. What a joy to be able to clean ourselves with real soap, and splash cold water all over our bodies. It was sheer bliss! We couldn't get enough of it.

One whole building had been put aside for this purpose. Rows of wooden cubicles ran along the walls. Each cubicle contained a *mandi* that was filled with cold water, similar to the one in our servants' quarters in Bandung. You were supposed to stand next to the tub on the slatted wooden floor and, with the aid of a tin bucket, scoop the water over yourself. The water simply ran away through the slatted floor. This way, the water in the tubs stayed clean for the next person. At least, that was the intention, but it did not always work out that way. The temptation was simply too much for some people. Many times they would climb right into the tub and were then caught floating ecstatically in the cold water. It was not the camp guards who got upset but the prisoners themselves. Big arguments erupted among the women about keeping the water clean for everyone.

In spite of the improved bathing conditions and food, our mother was finding it harder to function every day. We knew something had to be seriously wrong when one day she just refused to get out of bed. Since our father, as usual, was not around, we had to ask one of her friends to summon the camp nurse. Our mother was very ill indeed, with malaria, and needed to be isolated immediately. Since there was nowhere for her to go, no hospital or sick bay that wasn't already overflowing with critically ill patients, we children were placed in different quarters. Before we knew what was happening, we were hustled out of the room by a nurse and marched across the lawn to a building on the far side of camp. We were petrified, as the nurse was extremely strict, and forbade us to go back into our room for any reason.

Gijs was taken in by a friend of our mother's, as he was too young to be on his own. Unfortunately, she did not have the space to house Willem and me as well. We ended up in little cubbyholes, each so tiny that there was only room for one army cot. Nothing else. One small window at the top of the wall was the only source of light and air. It was so high up we couldn't even look out of it. We were expected to pass our days here until our mother recovered. It was like living in a cupboard.

Willem and I were devastated. I felt so utterly alone and abandoned, I cried myself to sleep every night. Willem and I tried to whisper to each other through the wooden partitions, but he felt as miserable as I did. During the day, as we sat outside the building where our mother lay in her hot little room, he and I planned how we would run away together until she was better and we could return to our own place. Where we were planning to go or how we would live I cannot remember, but it all seemed logical at the time.

The days were interminable and lonely. Willem and I were so in need of a kind word or some loving reassurance. I can't remember ever seeing my father at that time, in spite of our hanging about outside the barracks where our mother lay so desperately ill.

In the meantime, we asked anyone who came out of that building if they had seen our mother. Nobody ever had. Only the nurse went in and out of that room, and she never had time for us. All she would ever say was 'Be good, children! Go and play! You cannot see your mother!' as she dashed past us.

We became haunted by the dreadful thought that maybe her legs had finally burst open and she was lying up there in her little room dying without anybody knowing. One desperate day, when my longing to see her was more than I could stand, I crept up the stairs and stood outside her door. I listened intently to make sure there was no one in the room with her, and then I slowly and carefully opened the door and slipped inside. It was dark in the room, but I could see my mother lying on her cot with her eyes shut. I pushed the door closed behind me and sighed with happy relief to be with her again.

She heard me and opened her eyes. 'Claartje! What are you doing here?' she asked, stretching her hand out toward me.

I ran to her side and clung desperately to her arm. 'Can I come back? Are you better now? Are you going to die?' The words tumbled out as I hugged her tightly. With dread, I looked at her legs. Thank God, they were still there and in one piece. They hadn't burst open after all. I told her how relieved I felt about that, because I knew she would understand. She always did.

She asked me about Willem and Gijs and where we were staying. When I told her about the tiny cubbyholes that only held one bed, her face filled with sadness. She pulled herself up and, with her hands, lifted and pushed her swollen legs over the side of the cot.

'Go find Willem, please, and ask him to come see me.'

I was already halfway to the door.

'Oh, yes, and both of you bring your belongings back here with you.'

My heart beating wildly with joy, I flew out the door and down the dark stairs. It did not take me long to find Willem, who was as eager to see our mother as I was. Dashing into her room, he bumped right into the nurse, who had just come to check on her patient. She whirled around angrily and was just about to march us right back out the door when our mother stopped her.

'No, Nurse, they can stay. They are moving back in with me. I had no idea they were living all alone. I'm well enough now, and I want them here. I also want Gijs brought back.'

What wonderful words those were to us! That was the first night I slept well in a long time. Our family, which sadly did not include our father, was together again.

It was not long after moving back into our own stifling room that Willem, Gijs, and I came down with monkey pox. Similar to chicken pox, but brought on by malnutrition and squalid living conditions, it is a highly contagious disease. Hoping to prevent an outbreak of monkey pox, the head of the camp decided to transport us to the only hospital with beds available, even though it was quite a distance away. Willem, Gijs, and I were taken in an army ambulance that was so hot and so bumpy we were almost delirious by the time we got there. Our mother had not been able to accompany us, as there was no room in the back.

The hospital was a single-story building that had seen better days. It was obvious that no gardener had set foot on the premises since the war started. The grass was waist-high, and the bushes had grown up and over the windowsills. There was not a pane of glass in the windows, and the flies buzzed in and out in droves. The wards were filled to capacity, sometimes forcing two people to share a bed. Makeshift beds lined the hallways from the front doors all the way to the back. Gijs and I were put in one bed together, Willem's bed so close we could touch hands.

One long, narrow wooden table in the middle of the room served as an all-purpose workstation. Patients in need of washing were carried over to that table and laid on the bare wood. Chipped white enamel bowls with cold water for washing were brought over to you. If you were able, you washed yourself, right there in front of everyone in a mixed ward. If you were too sick, you waited until a nurse had the time to help you. Many a time I just lay there until my bones ached from pressing into the hard wood. A nurse would eventually pick me up and take me back to bed, unwashed. The next patient would then take a turn on the same table. If your hair happened to need washing really badly, the nurse would move you up to the top of the table until your head hung down over the end; then she poured cold water over your hair. The water collected in a basin on the floor, probably to be used again by the next patient. Water was very scarce.

At mealtimes, trays of food were brought to that same table and set down where, minutes before, a sick patient had lain. From there, the small bowls of rice would be taken to each patient in bed. Nurses simply set the bowls near you on the mattress in hopes that you would help yourself. In spite of Willem's valiant efforts to coax us into eating, neither Gijs nor I had the strength or desire to touch the rice. Willem would quickly devour both our servings, as well as his, before the nurses could take them away again. Either the nurses never knew or they simply didn't care. They had no time to worry about patients who couldn't make it on their own. As long as we were quiet, they weren't bothered, and Gijs and I were too weak to bother anyone.

One day, quite unexpectedly, I woke to see both our mother and father standing beside our beds. They had received no word of our condition since we left for the hospital, and had become so concerned that they managed to find transportation to come and see for themselves. I don't think our mother liked what she saw.

I looked over at Willem, who was sitting up in his bed, munching happily on the candies he'd been given. Our father then handed me a small purple basket with a lid, filled with my favorite jelly sweets. But I barely looked at them. I simply stood the basket between me and Gijs, who was still asleep.

'Aren't you going to eat one?' our mother asked as she felt my forehead and touched my burning cheeks.

I just looked at her, barely recognizing her, and closed my eyes, drifting in and out of sleep. I heard her ask first Willem, and then the nurses, if Gijs and I ever ate anything. The nurses explained that we were always given the food but that we never ate it. 'They are probably too ill' was their only explanation.

The next day our mother returned by herself. Having obtained a special pass to leave camp, she had made the long and arduous trek by bus. Starting early in the morning, she had waited in long lines for tickets, then had to transfer several times. The rickety old buses were uncomfortable and dirty. The broiling sun turned them into tin ovens, made worse by the many hot bodies pressed close against hers. She had crossed sluggish brown rivers teeming with mosquitoes and flies, and stopped in many *kampongs*, small villages, where more passengers crowded onto the already overloaded vehicle. By the time she reached the hospital in the afternoon, she was so exhausted and dehydrated she almost collapsed. But she was on a mission, and nothing was going to stop her. She had come to fetch us and take us home. She knew we were dying, and nobody seemed to care.

She walked slowly up to our beds as though she had come for a visit. Willem was very happy to see her again, and even more so when she told him to get up, as we were going home. Then, without another word, she picked me up under one arm and walked around to Gijs's side of the bed. Tucking him under her other arm, she walked calmly out of the ward. Nobody asked her where she was taking us or tried to stop her. Gijs and I had been fast asleep when she arrived, but we did not have the strength to complain about the mode of trans- portation. With her arms around our middles and our heads down, we dangled at her sides like limp rags as she plodded slowly back along the sandy path between the high grasses. The sun beat down, and our mother's arms were slippery with perspiration. A couple of times she sat us down in the shade of a tree and gave us all a drink from a bottle of water she had brought with her. She cooled our faces by wetting her hand and wiping it across our foreheads. Nobody spoke. The heat was too oppressive.

I do not remember the bus trip back to camp. Gijs and

I were so weak from the fever and starvation that we passed out several times. Willem fared a little better, as he had been able to eat in the hospital. But the long, hot trip back soon got the better of him and our mother as well.

It was night by the time we returned to camp. Our mother was so exhausted from having to carry us on and off buses all day long that she collapsed on the lawn in front of our barracks. The night was cool, and the stars were out. Most people had retired for the night, but a few still lingered to enjoy the cooler air. She laid us down on the grass and then lay down beside us. It was there that my father found us. He had searched all over the camp for her when he had returned from guard duty. He had no idea that she had gone all the way to the hospital to bring us home.

Recovery was painfully slow. Gijs and I refused to eat, as our stomachs could no longer accept food. We just wanted to be left alone to sleep.

'Don't give up now, my darlings,' our mother pleaded. 'It won't be much longer. We're nearly home.' She mashed bananas in our rice to make it more palatable and easier to swallow. Our poor mother spent hours patiently coaxing us to eat, one small teaspoon at a time, with long rests between. Little by little we regained our strength. Since we were still unable to walk, our mother would carry us down the stairs in the cool of the early morning and sit us in the shade of the trees, our backs against the trunks. From there we could watch the people passing. Occasionally someone would stop to chat. 'You must have just come out of hospital,' they'd say, as though that explained everything.

———

Since Margriet Kamp was a holding camp, it wasn't such a bad place. At least there were no hostile Japanese guards to watch out for constantly. With special passes, we could leave the camp and ride into town in a *betja,* a three-wheeled bicycle taxi. Everything was so amazing to us: the huge buildings, the shops, and the sidewalks crowded with people. Since we didn't have any money, we never bought anything. But we were free, and that was thrilling enough.

The worst thing about Margriet Kamp was the interminable wait for the transportation that would take us away from the misery of concentration camps. What could possibly be the cause of the holdup?

I was an adult with grown children of my own when I learned the reason behind our extended stay in Bangkok. Most of our family members and friends who had been in camps like us were already back in Holland. As time passed and there was no sign of our return, everyone started to grow concerned and began to question this delay. It so happened that a business acquaintance of our family, whose own wife and children were already safely back in Holland, heard of our dilemma and became quite disturbed. He told our family there that he had seen our father visiting plantations all over Java, following up on leads to purchase tea, coffee, and other products for his business. My mother was used to his frequent and extended trips away from camp, but she hadn't realized that he had not yet applied for passage home.

Ever the businessman, my father was more concerned with making deals than fighting for those hard-to-acquire transportation passes for his family. Luckily for us, this kind acquaintance took it upon himself to find out where we were and to secure passage home for us on the next available ship. We could have been home months before, sparing my mother more needless grief and hardship. I now understand full well her sadness and her sudden loss of interest in life. After all those years of struggling to keep us safe and fed, her husband's lack of concern for her and his family must have been a crushing blow. Yet not once did she ever say anything unkind about him to us.

17

Going Home

The months of waiting finally passed, and now, un-believably, here we were at last, climbing up the steep gangplank of the ocean liner *De Johan van Oldenbarnevelt,* which was going to take us back to Holland.

We had little to carry, as we possessed nothing but the clothes we were wearing, our precious painting of the flamboya tree, and the tattered Children's Bible. It really didn't matter. Nobody else had much to bring on board, either.

There was one notable exception: My mother was wearing a dress! A dark flowered dress with a small lace collar. She had been saving it since the beginning of the war for the day she was to go home. I couldn't take my eyes off her. She looked so pretty, with her curly hair cut short; and she had saved enough money from cutting other people's hair to buy herself some sandals.

In fact, we were all wearing shoes again. As we were returning to civilization, she had spent her hard-earned money on shoes for each of us. They were hard to get used to after all those years of going barefoot, but she was able to coax us into wearing them with her two favorite words: 'for Holland.' They worked like magic every time. Long before we ever reached our mother's homeland, however, we were already growing out of those shoes, and she had to cut holes for our toes to stick through.

She must have cut just about everybody's hair in camp. With the happy thoughts of going home at long last, people were anxious to spruce up. First on the list was a haircut.

And now that the time we had all dreamed about for so long had actually come, people streamed past us, pushing and shoving in their eagerness to get on board. Willem, Gijs, and I dashed up the gangplank after them. We were so excited. When we got on the boat, we stood aside and waited for our mother to come up. Holding on to the railings, she hobbled laboriously up the steep ramp on her swollen legs.

Looking down at her, it was not her legs I saw, or her struggle to keep her balance as people pushed past her, it was her smiling face. A smile of triumph and relief that she had made it and her children had made it, too. Only a few more steps and she would leave her life in the Dutch East Indies behind forever.

For the next four weeks, our new home was to be the cargo hold of this enormous ship, along with at least two thousand other passengers who were equally anxious to return to Holland. Mattresses had been strewn from wall to wall, like a thick striped rug with not an inch of space between, while hammocks swung overhead with the movement of the ship. We lay down wherever we could find a space, often sharing a mattress with a complete stranger.

Most people became seasick right at the start of the journey, so in no time the air was thick and rank with the acrid smell of vomit, sweating bodies, and urine-soaked mattresses.

Since the holds were several decks down in the bowels of the ship, they were airless and very hot. The lack of toilet facilities or even water taps made it necessary to climb the steep iron stairs to an upper deck. Most people who were trying to reach a railing over which to vomit into the sea never made it in time. The stairs soon became a dangerously slippery obstacle to fresh air. To get some relief from the stifling heat in the cargo holds, we all crowded onto the decks. This turned into a major problem when people started dragging mattresses up and turning the decks into sleeping quarters. This was absolutely forbidden.

My mother, Willem, Gijs, and I would try to stay up on deck as long as possible. With our backs leaning against one another and squeezed in between other people, we would watch for shooting stars and marvel at the phosphorescent trails left by the boat in the rolling ocean waves. The fresh air was wonderful, but there was a disadvantage to lingering. If you went back down into the hold too late, chances were that all the best, cleanest mattresses would be occupied. Nobody owned one particular area of their choice. Trying to lie down and fall asleep next to a stranger was difficult. The first person on the mattress usually took up most of the space, and some people were positively mean if woken up, albeit accidentally.

Many passengers were restless sleepers. Flailing and kicking, crying out in their nightmares, they rolled around from mattress to mattress so much that it was not at all surprising to wake up in a completely different area of the hold, surrounded by different people.

Shrill bells summoned us to meals. One of the cargo holds had been turned into a dining room, with rows upon rows of long, narrow tables and benches. At one end of each table sat the server, who was in charge of doling out the food, like our days in camp. We were expected to return to our own table for every meal.

The dining room was a depressing place, dark and dismal. Bare lightbulbs hanging over the tables threw off hardly enough light to show what you were eating. But it was the combination of many days' consolidated food smells that was the hardest to overcome. It seemed as though every meal that appeared on your plate tasted the same as the one from the day before, and the day before that. It was also in the dining room that people's manners were suddenly forgotten. Food, or the mere sight of it, brought out the worst in everyone. Meals were gulped down before the plate could be set down. Heaven forbid that one serving might have a couple more beans on it than another.

It got to the point that the bread basket could no longer be passed down the table because people would grab more than their fair share. Fights would ensue, with plates and mugs hurled across the dining room in fits of rage and frustration.

Inevitably some woman would start screaming and

crying uncontrollably at a table: another survivor who simply could take no more. Most people would be sympathetic toward her and sit her down, hugging her and assuring her that everything would be all right. She would bury her face in her hands and sob as though her heart would break. It was very unnerving to us to see the sadness, but my mother assured us the women would soon be all right again, and they usually were.

There was little for children to do on board. Willem usually wandered off in search of excitement and spent the day exploring the ship. It was so overcrowded that our mother tried to keep Gijs and myself close to her side. She was convinced that Gijs would fall overboard. As an active four-year-old he had no fear and would climb happily all over the railings. Many times he managed to sneak away and would be gone for hours, while our poor frantic mother searched high and low for him. She finally once again pinned a note to his shirt, requesting anyone who saw him wandering around to please return him to the life-buoy station on the rear deck.

———

Once we all got over our seasickness, we were able to appreciate the beautiful sights of the ocean. The sheer immensity of all that water heaving in giant waves around the boat. The whitecaps that looked like waves upon a wave, frothing past the portholes. Most wondrous of all were the flying fish leaping out of the sea as though racing with the ship. Dolphins, with their glistening blue backs, accompanied us for many miles on our journey home.

On calm days, lazy jellyfish sparkled like flowers in the dark blue waters. Every day brought something new, each more awe-inspiring than the next, but none more ominous than the albatross that arrived one day out of a clear blue sky.

People looked on with fear in their eyes as the big bird strutted clumsily around on deck.

'Oh my God!' they said. 'Shoo it away! Get rid of it!'

I did not understand what was so frightening about this bird, though I, too, kept my distance. It stayed on the boat for days, in spite of the valiant efforts of the sailors to make its life miserable.

'Don't you know? It means somebody is going to die,' Willem told me.

I didn't believe him, but I had gruesome visions of the albatross swooping down and carrying off some unsuspecting person on deck. For days I hung around below, preferring to lounge on the mattress rather than become the victim of the albatross. It wasn't until my mother was able to convince me that it was just a superstition, a fairy tale, that I was willing to return on deck. By then, the albatross had flown away.

There were few men on board, and our father was not among them. We had not seen him in weeks, and had to depart for Holland without saying good-bye since he was not around. We children were used to his absences, and didn't ask our mother about them. We sensed that she did not like to talk about him. We did enjoy talking to the young men on board who were returning from other concentration camps. There was one in particular we all grew very fond of. His name was Hans. He was returning to Holland, where his father was waiting anxiously for the return of his only son. This young man was so excited that he never stopped smiling or talking about the anticipated reunion. He had saved all his money and bought several gifts to take home. Every day he would talk about all the things he was going to do and whom he planned to visit. Just listening to him talk made us all feel glad to be alive and excited about the rest of our lives.

Then one day Hans didn't show up on deck. He must have overslept, we decided. Or maybe he was helping someone overcome a moment of despair. We didn't see

him all day, and it was as though we had lost our moti-
vating force. We hung around the deck where he liked
to sit, and kept asking everyone if they had seen him.
Finally we got word that Hans was in the sick bay,
seriously ill with pneumonia. Since he was not allowed
any visitors, everybody scribbled get-well messages on
any scraps of paper they could find and dropped them
into a cardboard box outside his room. Judging by the
many messages, he had touched the lives of nearly
everyone on board.

It was at dinner that night that the sad news of Hans's
death was announced. We were devastated. His burial
was to take place before the sun went down. We were
all on deck, struggling to understand how this could be,
when the stretcher with his body was brought up from
the sick bay. Covered with a beautiful embroidered cloth,
it was placed on some trestles near the railings. We craned
our necks to get one last glimpse of our special friend.
The captain stepped forward and asked everyone to join
him in saying a few prayers; then, as people wept, the
stretcher was lifted and one end placed on the railings.
Two sailors gently lifted the other end high into the air,
and our beloved Hans slowly slipped out from under the
cloth and disappeared forever into the cold, dark sea.
With tears in our eyes, we watched as the get-well

messages were sprinkled overboard and fluttered down
to his watery grave. We stood silently at the railing for
a long time, watching the white trail drifting away from
the boat as we continued our journey home without
him.

It was then, all at once, that I remembered the albatross.

Our dear friend's death signaled the beginning of daily
burials at sea. Sometimes there were three or four on
the same day. They usually took place early in the
morning when the sun first came up, or later in the
evening before the sun went down again. The sick bay
was overcrowded with patients, and only the most
serious cases were kept there. The others were being
cared for in the regular sleeping quarters, at one end of
the cargo hold.

It was May 1946, and in a few days it would be our
mother's birthday. If only there were something we
could give her. She had made quite a few friends on
board, as she was always talking to the women who sat
around her on the deck. I happened to mention to one

of them that it was going to be her birthday soon and wished I could find something special to give her. Much to my surprise, the woman knew immediately what I should make.

'I'll teach you to sew,' she said. 'I know she'd like that.'

We sat for the next several days, huddled together in a corner on the deck while she helped me make a tiny navy blue pouch embroidered with flowers. Into this we tucked a small religious card, decorated with a picture of a mother bird feeding her babies on a branch of apple blossoms. The text, in French, read, 'God feeds them, how much more are you better than the birds?' I must have taken that card out of its pouch a dozen times before I gave it to my mother, I loved it so much. I know that gift meant a lot to her, as I found it in one of her dresser drawers many years later, after she died in England.

We had by now been traveling several weeks across the Indian Ocean, into the Gulf of Aden, and were headed into the Red Sea. The sun beat down on us unmercifully every day. There seemed to be nowhere to get away from the heat. On deck you sat pressed against other perspiring bodies in the blazing sun, and down in the cargo holds it was like entering an oven where the air was so stale you thought you would choke.

As we were not allowed to bring the mattresses up on

deck, we all got used to sleeping where we sat. At least
at night the temperatures dropped enough to give some
relief from that heat. We were still wearing the same
clothes we had on the day we came on board, so none
of us looked any too fresh. My mother tried from time
to time to give the clothes a quick wash in the basin,
while we stood by so we could put them right back on.
The clothes felt wonderfully cool right after the cold-
water rinse, but they dried within a few minutes.

We were told that the boat was going to make a stop
in Port Said on the Suez Canal. The Red Cross had set
up immense tents of clothing that they were donating
to all the prisoners returning home. We were terribly
excited by the thought of new clothes. I still wanted a
red dress more than anything in the world.

Sailing up to and through the Suez Canal must have
been the hottest period of the whole trip. The canal
seemed to be carved right through the Arabian Desert,
miles of flat open sand through which the ship slowly
inched its way. What would happen, I wondered, if a boat
came through from the other end? We would certainly
collide. People ran alongside the boat on the stone walls.
We all watched in fascination as they shouted instructions and stood ready to catch the thick ropes that would
tie us up to the walls.

We were surprised to see a long train not far off, pulled by a steam engine standing on tracks that ran parallel to the boat. It was a rusty, primitive train without doors or glass in the windows. It was to take us inland to a place called Ataka, where the Red Cross had set up clothing stations and tents to supply us with all the necessities, such as soap, toothpaste, shampoo, and aspirin.

There was such a feeling of excitement on board as we crowded along the railings, jostling for a better view. We were all picturing ourselves in pretty new dresses, shoes, shirts, and underwear. Underwear? What a luxury!

I wanted ribbons. Red ribbons to match the red dress I was going to choose. I would wear the dress and ribbons when we got to Holland. I wanted to look pretty for my grandmother, whom I had never met.

An announcement came over the loudspeaker. We were all to move away from the railings and return to our regular places on deck. Since we couldn't all visit the clothing tents at the same time, our names would be called in alphabetical order. Those called were to line up near the gangplank and await further instructions. My heart sank. What if the first people took all the clothes? Why did we always have to be in the middle? Why couldn't they start with us for a change? I watched, scowling, as the first several hundred people made their way gingerly down to the shore and into the waiting train.

The train made many trips throughout the day, dropping off people at the tents in Ataka and returning immediately for more. The half-hour trip was hot and unpleasant. Chugging through arid wasteland, the engine billowed smoke into the windowless compartments as it struggled to gain speed, and swayed dangerously from side to side on its aging springs.

It was many days of excruciating waiting at the railings before our name was finally called. My heart was pounding with excitement as we pushed our way into the throng heading down the gangplank and into the train. Finally I was going to get my red dress and red ribbons and who know what else. Maybe even some red shoes. Every day I had watched as people returned, arms laden with clothes. I scrutinized as many bundles as I could to see if anybody had my red dress.

I did not see a single red dress draped over anyone's arms, but I also failed to see just what kinds of clothes they were carrying. Now, as I waited at the entrance to the tents for my mother to catch up, I craned my neck around the people in front of me to catch a glimpse of the 'dress table.' A voice over the loudspeakers was booming out instructions. Nobody could enter until everyone was assembled. We were then to proceed in an orderly fashion to the various areas, where we were entitled to one item of each type of clothing. One winter coat, one pair of shoes, one sweater, blouse, skirt, warm hat and mittens, socks, and of course a change of underwear. For the boys there would be pants and shirts.

What about dresses? Weren't there any dresses? Surely there must be dresses, I whined, they simply forgot to mention them. My mother lost her patience. The heat under those awnings was so intense, and she was having such a struggle pushing our sweating arms into the sleeves of heavy winter coats or woolen sweaters, that we almost left without any clothes at all. It was a long and arduous task. The tables were heaped high with every assortment of sizes and colors. Red Cross personnel tried as best they could to help with the sizes. Colors and style were immaterial, just so long as everyone had something warm to wear when we arrived in Holland.

The closest I got to a red dress was a dingy maroon coat. All the joy and excitement of choosing clothes was gone. The extreme heat and the jostling bodies, pulling and shoving through the mountains of clothes, frayed everyone's tempers. Children were crying as exhausted mothers tried to squeeze their hot, swollen feet into uncomfortably stiff shoes. Since my mother had three children and herself to outfit, we were under the tents for most of the day. Finally, laden with bags of clothes, we staggered back to the waiting train and sank gratefully onto its hard wooden benches. We sat in numb silence, staring out at the passing landscape as we slowly headed back to the boat. After all those days of anticipation, the day had been a heartbreaking disappointment. My poor mother was so exhausted that she had to be helped back up the gangplank by a couple of sailors. That night we collapsed onto the deck and stayed there until the following morning.

———

The boat stayed in Port Said for about a week. We were thankful to get on our way again, through the Mediterranean Sea, around the Rock of Gibraltar, and into the North Atlantic Ocean. It was about this time that Willem became seriously ill. He was confined to the sick bay, and only our mother could go in to see him. Though she tried her best to assure me that he would soon be better, I was convinced that the albatross had something to do with his illness.

The days dragged on, and still more people were buried at sea every day. I attended every funeral, as I wanted to make sure that it wasn't Willem being buried.

There really was no way I could have known, as each body was always tied into a body bag, but it made me feel better to be there.

A terrible storm in the Bay of Biscay kept everyone below-decks. The combination of the heaving seas and the putrid air in the cargo holds ensured that not a single person was spared from becoming violently seasick. We were all beginning to wonder whether any of us would make it to Holland. People lay around listlessly on urine-damp mattresses. It wasn't that no one tried to make it to the toilets in time; most of the time it happened while you were asleep, 'from sheer nerves,' my mother used to say.

Everyone suffered from nightmares. You'd wake up screaming in terror, paralyzed by the terrifying dreams that haunted you every night. Some people took to racing crazily around in the dark, stumbling over sleeping bodies in their anxiety to get away from the horror in their dreams. My brothers and I were so rest-less that, in spite of starting off the night close together, we always ended up scattered all over the hold by the morning.

Willem never did make it out of sick bay for the rest of the trip. I was so desperately worried about him, I was convinced that he was dying and nobody would tell me. My mother got special permission for me to see him from the sick bay doorway. Ill with double pneumonia, he lay under a pile of blankets and was not allowed to move. Looking pale and haggard, his eyes closed, he did not look like the same Willem who always knew what was going on and was always involved in some adventure. In a few days we would be arriving in Holland. Would he be able to leave the boat and come with us?

We had been at sea for a total of four or five weeks when Holland first came into sight. A mighty cheer went up, and people hugged one another with tears in their eyes. Dancing around on deck, they sang the 'Wilhelmus,' the national anthem, and pointed and laughed or simply broke down and cried. I stood at the railing and stared at this land of our dreams. This land that had figured in so many conversations and stories. This land that kept us going when times got unbearable.

All I felt was disappointment. Total and utter disappointment. Where was the snow I had heard so much about? The windmills and farmers in wooden shoes and women in pretty dresses and white hats? I had imagined sliding on the snow and skating on the canals. Was none of that true after all?

As we neared, people on the docks were waving and

shouting. Many were waving large Dutch flags and carrying bouquets of flowers. The passengers around me were breaking down and weeping loudly. No one else seemed disappointed with this Holland.

To my relief, my mother told me that all the patients from the sick bay and their families were going to leave the ship before everyone else. As the crowd on deck stood aside, the stretchers were brought up. Willem was covered from head to toe, so I couldn't really see him, but his name was printed on a label pinned to one of the blankets. As soon as his name was called out by one of the sailors, our mother grabbed our hands and we followed the stretcher down the gangplank. I was holding tightly on to our little suitcase tied up with string. The only thing inside it was the painting of the flamboya tree. Tears were streaming down my mother's face as she shouted good-bye to the friends she had made on board. She walked slowly and carefully on wobbly, painful legs until we reached the spacious hangars where the stretchers were lined up on cement floors. Bending over, she uncovered a portion of the blanket to check how Willem was doing. His face was flushed and his eyes were closed.

'We're here, Willem. We're in Holland. We've made it!' she breathlessly whispered as she stroked his face.

He gave a little smile as he opened his eyes. "That's good, Mum. We made it,' he answered weakly.

Outside, the remaining passengers were streaming into the waiting arms of family or friends, joyously hugging and crying after all these years of uncertainty. Still others were rushing to the trains and buses that would take them on the final lap of their journey to freedom.

More and more stretchers were brought from the ship, till the whole hangar was filled with desperately ill patients all waiting for ambulances to take them either to hospitals or to their homes. There were so many patients that the wait was long, but we were used to waiting, to standing in lines and not expecting anything. The difference here was that everyone was so kind, bringing us water and food; they couldn't do enough for us. A chair was brought for my mother and a crate on which to rest her legs. A doctor hovered anxiously around and asked her several times if there was something he could do to make her more comfortable. Every time he asked her, she looked at him with such surprise that he finally laughed and said, 'You're in Holland now. We're going to look after you.'

She smiled gratefully and looked away with tears in her eyes. It had been a long, long time.

When the ambulances finally arrived, as many of us as would fit inside and were traveling in the same direction crowded in. A special seat was cleared for my mother. Gijs and I sat side by side on a bench with one of the ambulance crew. He kept looking at us and then at our mother and shaking his head in disbelief.

'How long were you there?' he asked.

'Almost four years,' our mother answered.

'Disgusting! Dirty Japs!' he mumbled as if to himself. For a while we rode along in silence.

'Where are you going now?' he asked.

'To our grandmother's house,' Gijs and I told him. 'She's waiting for us.'

18

Starting Over

I can't in all honesty say that being back in Holland was everything we had dreamed it would be. Of course it was wonderful living in a beautiful, clean house with someone who was genuinely concerned about whether we had enough to eat or drink, but we were scared. Being scared had been such a part of our lives for so many years that it was hard not to fear every new experience. Settling in became another battle of wills.

Now that we were back in Holland, a country that my brothers and I had never lived in before, our grandmother simply expected us to put the war years behind us and grow up like well-behaved Dutch children. As far as she was concerned, there was nothing to be scared of in her house. Didn't we know that? Why did we jump at every loud noise, for goodness' sakes? And as far as our eating habits were concerned, they were an abomination! You'd have thought that anyone who had been starved as long as we had would be only too glad to have all the good food that she served every day.

She had scrimped and saved her ration cards for months when she heard we were alive and would be coming to stay with her. Times were tough in Holland, too, and food was still scarce. She wanted there to be plenty to feed us all.

No matter how hard my mother tried to explain that our stomachs had shrunk to such an extent that we could not eat more than a couple of spoonfuls per meal, we knew that our grandmother felt deeply offended. She absolutely forbade us to drink water before or during a meal, as she was convinced that this was the reason we couldn't eat the food. Little did she realize that we couldn't eat the food without the water, as that was what we had to do in camp in order to feel full at mealtimes. The water made the rice swell in our stomachs and satisfied our hunger.

We also found her food hard to swallow. It was as though our very throats had contracted. We would almost choke on meat or hard vegetables, and any medication or vitamins had to be crushed between two spoons and then washed down with a little water.

There was one meal, however, that I absolutely loved, and if it was cut up small enough, I did my best to eat it without water just to please her. It was smoked eel.

As soon as she realized my passion for smoked eel, my grandmother used this as a tool for bribery. It was not that she was cruel or unkind. On the contrary. She wanted us to eat and grow healthy, and she was going to do whatever it took. Our thin, bony bodies and rotting teeth upset her no end.

I will never forget the day we sat down for lunch and I could smell the smoked eel that I knew was in the covered dish. It stood in the middle of the table next to a basket of bread. Nothing else. No cheese, no butter, no salad. None of the usual items that made up a regular lunch. What did surprise me were the glasses of water. We never had water at the table. I took several sips and waited expectantly for the eel to be divided onto our plates.

'You may all take a slice of bread,' my grandmother said as she removed the silver lid from the dish. With a fork she placed the eel on her plate. I watched her every move, my mouth watering in anticipation.

'I'm sorry,' she said, 'but you are not going to get any of this. You are just going to eat bread and water until you learn to eat everything that is put on your plates. You have to realize that you cannot eat only what you like.'

I was dumbfounded and cried silently in my chair. I cannot remember the rest of that miserable meal, but I do know that it took a long time before we were able to eat the kinds of meals that pleased her.

The first several months after our arrival in Holland were the hardest for all of us. It was as though the shock of seeing how starved and sickly we were made my grandmother angry. Why hadn't we tried to escape? Surely we could have gotten off the island before the Japanese invaded? She repeated the same questions over and over again. At first my mother tried to explain how impossible that had been. That they had never believed it was going to get that bad until it was too late. But my grandmother couldn't accept those answers until my mother asked her why it would have been any better in Holland. Life had been extremely difficult after Hitler invaded. So difficult, in fact, that no one wanted to hear the stories about the Japanese concentration camps. They had enough bad stories of their own. No one, that is, except my grandmother. She wanted to hear the stories and hoped by listening to them that she could ease some of the hurt in our young lives.

Once she knew that we were settling down, our mother went to Switzerland to recover from her malnutrition and also to become reacquainted with our father, who had joined her there. His neglect in Bangkok had hurt her very deeply. How could he leave us to languish hopelessly in camp when we could have been on our way home? This was so incomprehensible to her that their relationship never fully recovered. After the first joys of finding each other in the same camp, our mother realized quite quickly that her husband had changed. Even we children realized it. Though he had never been an overly affectionate father before the war, he had been fun, as he was never as strict as our mother. But now he could hardly be bothered with us. The cruel, intervening war years had put a great distance between us, and we no longer felt much affection for this man who was never around for us anyway. We were well aware, too, of the recent tension between our parents.

Did our mother already know at this time about our father's affair with a nurse while we were still in the concentration camp? She told me once that he was always talking about how well this nurse had looked after him. For our mother it must have seemed as though her years of misery were far from over. The rest of the family was hoping that their prolonged stay in Switzerland could heal the rift that the war had brought about.

Life wasn't any more joyful for us children than it was for our parents. With our mother's departure to Switzerland, our grandmother was now left fully in charge of three very sick young children. Willem was unable to shake himself free of the double pneumonia he had arrived with, and grew weaker by the day. Then Gijs and I both came down with it as well. Our grandmother was a strict nurse, and I was convinced that she had eyes in the back of her head and peepholes in every wall. Though it was summer, she made us lie under several layers of blankets, with only our heads sticking out. It never failed to amaze us how she knew when we pulled our arms from under the covers and laid them on top.

'Cover up, Claartje!' she would shout to me from the next room. 'Gijs, lie down!'

With time and a lot of patience, though, our bodies healed, and, to our grandmother's delight, our appetites improved. We seldom wet our beds anymore, or cringed when we heard footsteps on the gravel paths around the

Holland, winter 1946. I am wearing the maroon coat
received in Port Said from the Red Cross.

house. After weeks and weeks of patiently picking out
the lice, one at a time, our grandmother pronounced
our scalps pink and clean. We also began to sleep through
the night without screaming in terror from our nightmares. The nightmares continue to haunt me to this day,

though over the years they have become much less frequent.

We all recovered from pneumonia and grew stronger under our grandmother's loving, watchful eyes. During

My brothers and me in Holland, 1946.

the months that followed, we slowly shared our experiences of the concentration camp with her. A strong bond of affection and mutual admiration grew out of those talks. She was a wonderful listener and encouraged us to tell her everything. In the process we began to heal not only our bodies but also our minds.

19

The Final Chapter

I wrote this book as a tribute to my beloved mother, who never gave up on her family and the ultimate struggle to survive. Though she battled daily to keep us fed and clean, I never heard her complain about or curse those who made our lives so miserable. I'm sure her heart ached when she saw our hungry faces and listened to our pleas for just a little more food, as she always managed to find an extra morsel she could share from her own plate.

Her strong will to survive against all odds helped us children to accept our difficult lives until something better came along. She never dwelled on what could have been or should have been, though she did try to keep our hopes up that better times lay just ahead. I'm sure that for her own sake, too, she felt she had to keep positive thoughts, as it would have been so easy to give up. She longed for this burden to be lifted from her shoulders.

Her expectations of us as honest, kind, and well-mannered children never wavered. She was extremely proud of us, and she wanted her husband to be proud, too, when the time finally came to reestablish our family life. She always carefully preserved her dreams for the future.

Life after the war, though, was much more difficult than she had anticipated. I'm sure she felt terribly let down.

She returned from Switzerland much healthier, and also pregnant. This was the last thing she had expected from a body that was so malnourished and sickly, but it filled her with the hope that the new life growing inside her meant that her own life was turning around for the better as well. She was filled with joy the day she told her parents-in-law about the new baby, and she was dumbfounded when her happy news was received with anger and disgust.

'How could you be so careless? Couldn't you have been more careful? What were you thinking?'

It made her feel dirty and cheap and sad, as though it was solely her fault and had nothing to do with her husband, their own son.

Unlike my grandparents, I couldn't have been more delighted. I wanted a sister so badly, it was all I could think of. Every day I prayed fervently for a sister, making promises to God, which, if I had been able to carry them all out, would certainly have assured me of sainthood. God did come through, I'm happy to say, and gave me

The whole family upon our return, once more, to Ceylon, in 1948 (left to right): Gijs; Willem (standing); a new sister, Helena; my mother; me; my father.

the sister I had prayed for. In spite of everyone's concerns, Helena was a big, beautiful, and healthy baby, and nothing could diminish my love for her, not even my grandparents' comment that I was now no longer the only girl in the family.

After one year in Holland, our whole family returned to Ceylon. Willem and I continued to struggle in school, as we were desperately behind in our academic studies, a situation aggravated further by the fact that we could not speak English.

Unfortunately, the relationship between my parents began to deteriorate drastically, as my father spent more and more time away from home 'on business.'

We stayed in Ceylon for three years, during which time my mother realized that her marriage was not going to work out after all. It was a numbing blow to her dreams, not only for herself but also for her children, who, she felt, deserved a normal life.

Our family moved to England, where my father opened his head office in London, and Willem, Gijs, and I were sent to boarding schools.

Our mother filed for divorce, and after a bitter, drawn-out proceeding, she gained full custody of us four children. Having brought us safely through those long war years by herself, she was certainly not going to allow our father to have any say in our upbringing now. She knew she was capable of doing a very good job by herself.

Finally, it seemed she could get on with her life.

She loved living in England and bought herself a little old farmhouse in the country, surrounded by fields and meadows, where she could raise chickens and goats, vegetables, roses and lilacs, and play her beloved violin to her heart's content. She acquired many music students for violin and piano lessons, conducted her own women's choir, and played in a local orchestra led by Benjamin Britten. A small silver tray was inscribed with her name and dedicated to her after her death, as a trophy to be won yearly by choral groups in the region of East Anglia, England. How I wish she could have been honored while she was alive. It would have meant so much to her.

She was often asked to give talks about her life in the concentration camp. Though we rarely discussed the camp among ourselves – 'That's in the past. Get on with your life' – she gladly gave talks to other people. She liked to stress how good life was now. How lucky we were. How precious each day was.

All four of her children married and gave her many grandchildren whom she adored and was so proud of. Her life was full and satisfying. She was happy at last.

As for my father, he, too, settled in England and got remarried. Was this the nurse from the war years? I think it was. It was not a happy marriage, and I sincerely believe that he regretted what had happened between him and my mother. He would invite me out to dinner when I was working in London and ask me how my mother was doing and whether she was happy. At that time I didn't feel he had a right to know just how happy she was. He had hurt her so much in the past, I could never forgive him. None of us children ever grew close enough to him to inform him of our marriages and subsequent grandchildren. He died a lonely man in his early fifties, after several strokes.

Though he always vowed, after witnessing our parents' bitter relationship, that he would never get married and have children, my brother Willem married in his early twenties and was soon the loving father of three children. He made the British army his career. He left the army to take care of our mother when she became ill, then moved his family to Toronto, Canada, after her death. He is now retired.

My brother Gijs was the adventurer. Whether traveling in the Amazon Basin and living with the Surinee

Indians on the river Tocantins, or deep-sea diving in the North Sea, he could not settle down until the day he bought a Dutch barge and sailed it back to England. The barge became his home and livelihood, and he married and had two daughters. He recently sold the barge, and he and a close friend bought a wonderful and historic old pub, the Ship Inn, in Blaxhall, Suffolk, not far from where we grew up.

My sister, Helena, married at a very young age and soon had four children. After getting divorced about fifteen years later, she bought and ran a large guesthouse in a popular seaside resort.

As for myself, I met my American husband in Toronto, Canada, where we were both working at the time. He had two young children from a former marriage and he and I both agreed, after some time, that they needed a mother. We got married and added to the family with two more children and then moved to the United States. We are now enjoying life with our many grandchildren, among whom we proudly include a set of triplets. Life really is good.

I wish with all my heart that I could say my mother lived happily ever after, but that was not to be. Just when life showed so much promise, she became ill with a very fast-growing cancer and died within six months at the age of fifty-six.

Up to the end, she never complained. I'm sure she never even considered the unfairness of life, as she was always so grateful for all she had. She always assured us children that she would live forever. And in our hearts she does.

We'd often look up and find her studying our faces. When we'd ask her why, she'd answer simply, 'I like to look at you. I love you so much.'

I have the painting of the flamboya tree now, and it hangs in my home from the same cloth cord that was used in camp. Far from making me feel sad when I look at it, it reminds me of my mother and the joy this painting gave her, and the strength to carry on.

I wish we could have spent more time together. I miss my mother very much. I'm sorry I never thanked her for bringing us all safely through the most horrendous time of our lives with so much love and strength and that no-nonsense attitude of hers.

I will never forget her spirit and courage, and therefore dedicate this book to her with all my love and admiration.

Thank you, Mum. I love you.

Acknowledgments

If it had not been for my husband's insistence to 'Write it down!' this book may never have been written. I thank Jerry from the bottom of my heart for his enthusiasm and endless patience, and for all the wonderful meals he learned to cook while I worked on 'The Book!'

Special thanks go to Earl Inman, in Damariscotta, Maine, who taught me how to start sifting through all the memories, and also to Sara Stamey, in Bellingham, Washington, who professionally reviewed the manuscript and encouraged me to 'Get it out there!'

I will always be grateful to Janis Donnaud, my agent in New York, who believed in this book right from the start and knew just where to take it. Thank you, Janis.

For her sensitive guidance and advice in the fine-tuning of the manuscript, I particularly want to thank Pamela Cannon, my editor. I learned so much from her, I'd like to do it all over again.